INCLUDING
the EARTH
IN OUR
PRAYERS
A Global Dimension to Spiritual Practice

A Revised and Updated Edition
of *Awakening the World*

INCLUDING *the* EARTH IN OUR PRAYERS

A Global Dimension to Spiritual Practice

LLEWELLYN VAUGHAN-LEE

THE GOLDEN SUFI CENTER

First published in the United States in 2019 by
The Golden Sufi Center
P.O. Box 456, Point Reyes, California 94956.
www.goldensufi.org

©2019 by The Golden Sufi Center.
Second edition of *Awakening the World: A Global Dimension to
Spiritual Practice* ©2006 by The Golden Sufi Center.

Printed and bound in the USA
Cover design by Anat Vaughan-Lee.

ISBN:
 978-1-941394-30-4 *(paperback)*
 978-1-941394-31-1 *(ePub)*
 978-1-941394-32-8 *(pdf)*
 978-1-941394-33-5 *(kindle)*

Library of Congress Cataloging-in-Publication Data

Names: Vaughan-Lee, Llewellyn, author.
Title: Including the earth in our prayers : a global dimension to
spiritual practice / by Llewellyn Vaughan-Lee.
Other titles: Awakening the world
Description: Second [edition]. | Point Reyes Station, California
: Golden Sufi Center, 2019. | Rev. ed. of: Awakening the world
: a global dimension to spiritual practice. 2006. | Includes
bibliographical references and index.
Identifiers: LCCN 2019000386 | ISBN 9781941394304 (pbk. :
alk. paper) | ISBN 9781941394311 (epub) | ISBN 9781941394335
(mobi (kindle))
Subjects: LCSH: Spiritual life.
Classification: LCC BL624 .V378 2019 | DDC 297.4/4--dc23
LC record available at https://lccn.loc.gov/2019000386

CONTENTS

PREFACE

Including the Earth in Our Prayers (first published in 2006
as *Awakening the World*) is the fifth in a series of six books
originally written between 2000 and 2006 about the
awakening consciousness of oneness and what this means
for humanity and the Earth.[1] If there are repetitions of
themes or ideas either within individual books or within
this series, it is deliberate. The intention behind these
books is not just to convey ideas or teachings, but to weave
together a tapestry about the spiritual transition of this
time. Certain themes—like the consciousness of oneness,
the suffering and awakening of the Earth, the union of
inner and outer worlds, the magic of life, and spiritual
consciousness as a catalyst for change—are central threads
in this tapestry. Together they form a spiritual foundation
for the shift from a story of separation to a story of life's
multihued unity.

From what is small and fragile
let abundance and power come:
let humanity take on
the consciousness
of the whole of creation
and be absorbed
by
this task.[2]

PREFACE
TO NEW EDITION

When I was seventeen I was traveling alone in the Far East and fell seriously ill. I remember being taken in and cared for by a group of young people, who had been strangers but soon became friends. We were connected by the simple belief that love and music could change the world, that war could become peace, and humanity awaken to a new way of being. I can still remember George Harrison's song, "My Sweet Lord," playing endlessly like a *mantra* on the radio in my sickroom, a symbol of the hope and unity of the time.

Of course we were idealistic. The Vietnam War was to drag on for four more years. Genocides in Bosnia and Rwanda would follow, Syria would be destroyed by a civil war killing hundreds of thousands. But for a moment there were these seeds of a future that is still waiting—a future born of love and unity, and a spiritual awakening that belongs to all. Maybe this awakening of the world will remain as a dream, just a song heard for an instant and then lost, drowned by the clamor of our materialistic culture as it continues its ecocide, destroying the fragile web of life with its endless greed and desires. Or maybe it can come alive, spring returning after a bleak winter of forgetfulness, the music of the sacred heard again, the oneness that belongs to all of creation felt as the simple joy of life.

When I came back to Europe I entered a world very different to the grey streets of my childhood. I discovered spiritual practice and spiritual friends. This was when spiritual paths from Tibet, India, and the Middle East arrived in the West, when orange-robed *sannyasi* could be seen dancing down Oxford Street in London, and aspiring dervishes whirled and chanted newly learned *dhikrs*. Spirituality was alive in all of its colors and sounds, the smell of incense everywhere. But sadly, or inevitably, the simple joy of this awakening became diluted as spirituality was brought into the marketplace, and rather than a celebration of oneness—the Divine as the ground of our being—spiritual practices became focused on self-transformation. Self-development became more popular than selfless service. And so a central ingredient became distorted or lost—the basic spiritual truth that "it is not about me." The renunciation of self, or in Rûmî's enigmatic words, "there is no dervish, or if there is that dervish is not there," would find little place in the marketplace of spirituality. As one friend said to me years later, "How can Sufism become popular in America, when it is all about becoming nothing?"

Many spiritual practices—meditation, mindfulness, living in the moment—are of great benefit for our individual journey of self-transformation. They can bring harmony, peace, stillness, lessen the stress in our hectic lives. But, without this central note they cannot realize their true potential, the real experience of the oneness of divine love. And there is a sadder aspect to this story which is not so well known in the West. Real spiritual practice is never for ourself alone, but always for the whole, always for the sake of the Beloved. And if we limit our practice within the horizon of our own separate self, we deny life a primal nourishment, an essential quality of love and light. We starve the Soul of the World of a spiritual energy it needs for its regeneration and evolution. This was always understood by shamans and Indigenous wisdom keepers, such as the Kogi Mamas whose work with *Aluna*,[1] the force behind nature, is to keep the world in balance.

In the summer of love and the few years that followed, we were given a dream, brothers and sisters of all races coming together, oneness alive. Like all dreams it faded "into the light of common day," but now, as the Earth is dying, species depleted, oceans full of plastic, as our cultures seem caught in divisiveness, there is a calling to return to the spark that gave birth to that dream. To awaken to the global song of unity, which I first felt when cared for in a strange land by friends who were strangers. And we need to include the Earth Herself in this prayer of love. She who gave us birth, who has nourished us with Her endless generosity, whom we have raped and desecrated, is unbalanced, sick, and needs our care and attention.

In the decade and a half since I wrote the first version of this book about a global dimension to spiritual practice, titled *Awakening the World*, there has been an emerging movement that links together spiritual practice, unity consciousness, and care for the Earth. Spiritual Activism and Subtle Activism are different expressions of this movement. Subtle Activism is about using consciousness-based practices for collective transformation, while a spiritual activist means "working to create a loving, just, sacred, and sustainable world through means that are also loving, just, sacred, and sustainable."[2] With different voices they speak the same truth: we can no longer afford to limit our loving to the personal, our spiritual practice to individual development.

Love and care are what calls us. If I have learned anything in half a century of spiritual practice, it is the power of love. We need to reawaken to the power of love in the world. It is our love for the Earth that will heal what we have desecrated, that will guide us through this wasteland, helping our dying Earth to regenerate, and help us to bring light back into our darkening world. Love links us all together in the most mysterious ways, and love can guide our hearts and hands. The central note of love is oneness. Love speaks the language of oneness, of unity rather than separation.

Love and care—care for each other, care for the Earth—are the simplest and most valuable human qualities. And love belongs to oneness. We know this in our human relationships, how love draws us closer, and in its most intimate moments we can experience physical union with another. It can also awaken us to the awareness that we are one human family, even as our rulers become more authoritarian, our politics more divisive. And on the deepest level, love can reconnect us with our essential unity with all of life, with the Earth Herself.

This book tells a story of love and prayer, how spiritual practice is not just for ourselves, our own journey, but for life itself. It reminds us how to live this love, how the inner and outer worlds[3] work together, how the individual is a microcosm of the whole, how the Soul of the World sings. It steps back to reclaim the ancient spiritual teachings of our ancestors, and then relates this wisdom to the need of our present time. It suggests ways in which this energy and transformative potential of our spiritual nature can be applied today, when humanity is at a tipping point and the Earth Herself is crying for our help. How can we take real responsibility for a world in crisis, and help Her to awaken? We are the place where love can be born, where the prayer for the Earth can be heard.

—Llewellyn Vaughan-Lee,
November 2018

INTRODUCTION

When one is changing,
How does one know
a change is taking place?
When one is not changing,
How does one know that a change
hasn't already occurred?
Maybe you and I are still
in a dream and
have not yet awakened.

Chuang Tsu

We are living in a time of fundamental change, a period of increasing divisiveness, tribalism, isolationism, even as a global consciousness of unity struggles to be born. We are a part of these changes, and yet these changes also depend upon us. Everything is interdependent in the inner and outer worlds. And our spiritual practice is an essential, if little understood, catalyst for this change. Our spiritual practice, our aspiration and awareness, are part of the lifeblood of the planet. There is an urgency now, a primal need, that we *live* the depths of our true nature, our desire for what is Real. Life is calling to us to realize our essential self and life's wholeness. We are needed to help life to awaken from a dream that is destroying it.

But if we are to live the real potential of our spiritual practice, we need to break free from the focus on our own individual journey. We need to reclaim the simple truth that spiritual life is "not about us," and open to a larger, all-embracing vision. If spiritual life is not about the whole, it has lost its true nature; it has instead been subverted by the ego and its patterns of self-concern. Everything that has been created is in service to life, to the real purpose of creation. This belongs to the "Original Instructions"[1] that were given to the earliest wisdom keepers. We are not separate from each other or from life, and we need to recognize how our individual spiritual journey, our praise and thanksgiving, are part of life's sacred purpose and can nourish life in different ways.

Just as the individual can forget her true nature and real purpose, as many of us have painfully experienced, so can life itself forget. Life is an interdependent living organism that embodies the collective consciousness of humanity. As humanity has become addicted to materialism and forgotten the sacred nature of life, so is life forgetting its own sacred nature, its primal purpose of divine revelation. We need to redeem this desecration, give back to the Earth an awareness of its sacred nature. This is the work of the lover, the spiritual traveler, the one who is drawn to the core of life, to the mystery of love and service. We carry within our spiritual centers the secrets of life, and we know the deep joy in recognizing what has been hidden within the heart. Part of our purpose is to give these secrets back to life: to help life reawaken to its true nature.

Our individual spiritual journey is part of the world's journey. To deny this is to live inside the veil of separation. A simple awareness of oneness unites us with all of life, with every stone, every insect, every soda can crumpled in the garbage. We are life itself, breathing, suffering, rejoicing. We are the pain of the sick and the laughter of the child. We are neither better nor worse than any particle of creation. Our hunger for the Source, our search for the Divine, is life's hunger, life's search. We need to give our journeying back to life and acknowledge the oneness that unites everything. Nothing is separate. All is One. To take this step is to renounce many of our spiritual expectations. How often have we hoped that our journey would free us from life's difficulties, hoped to be something special, to be other than the ordinary, even to become "enlightened?" The ego tries to claim everything for itself, even subverting the soul's longing for God into another illusion. Do we have the courage to give up these illusions, our spiritual dreams, to step into the arena of real spiritual service? Can we leave behind this seductive but limited imagined spirituality and embrace the real unknown? Do we dare to know what life and love really want from us, the vulnerability and complete participation that are needed? Here there is no bargaining, no safe place, but a giving of oneself without expectations: a response to a need that is present in every breath. Life needs our spiritual commitment; otherwise it will die, destroyed by greed and materialism, by a culture that thinks only of itself.

Every breath can be an awareness of the Divine, of the sacred within us and under our feet. Living this simple but primary awareness in our daily life—when we wash the dishes and take out the garbage, when we read our children to sleep—we nourish life on the deepest level. We are then present at the core of creation, where the sacred takes on form, where our remembrance is part of the lifeblood of the planet. Life needs this as much as a drowning man needs air.

And yet centuries of spiritual history tell us to turn away from life, to seek only the inner journey and renounce the outer world. Religions tell us of the darkness and dangers of our instinctual nature, of our bodies, of how we can become so easily seduced and corrupted by the world. These are stories of our forefathers, and while they contain truths, these teachings belong to a time that has passed. We cannot escape from the demands of the present. We cannot be deaf to life's pressing need. To be awake is to respond to the need of the moment, and in this moment the world needs us. Can we deny the call of the Soul of the World, of the Earth which is crying?

The Earth needs our prayers and practices, the light of our spiritual aspiration. Just as Her waters are made toxic, air polluted, so is the sacred light of Her soul fading. Her cry is both for our hands and hearts, for our love and care. This is a calling to those whose are awake to bring together heaven and earth, spirit and matter, to remember that every step is sacred.

When we respond to life's call for us to open our hearts and remember the sacred, we will discover that the ancient spiritual truths are also alive and changing, revealing a new face. The spiritual journey is not a text written in an old book, but is part of the divine mystery of life. Our longing for God and the journey Home are at the core of creation. They are part of the heartbeat of life. Without the stream of souls turning towards God, life would lose a quality of music and sacred meaning. But as the oneness of life changes and evolves, so does the way the journey presents itself. It is always the same journey, the eternal cry of the soul for its source, the lament of the reed torn from the reed-bed. But now the journey needs to acknowledge life's oneness and the interdependence of all of creation. Oneness needs to be stamped into the cells of the wayfarer, so that from the very beginning of the journey, from the moment we turn towards the light, we honor the whole. We need to bring our soul's turning towards God into the cells of our body, into the breath that connects us with all of life. We can no longer afford to separate the inner from the outer, the one from the many. The path is changing. Doors in the inner worlds that used to open us to mystical secrets are being closed, while other doorways, often in the midst of life, are being opened. The path is also revealing deeper truths that until now have been kept hidden. There are spiritual teachings, ancient traditions, that have always connected the inner journey to the whole of life, that have kept the balance between the inner and outer worlds and used spiritual practices as a way of nourishing the whole. Indigenous wisdom keepers hold some of these teachings. Other practices will gradually be revealed, their esoteric dimension adapted to the present time. Part of the purpose of this book is to point to this dimension of spiritual practice—to show, for example, how the axis of love functions at the center of the world, and how the heart connects together different levels of reality.

For centuries these have been closely guarded secrets, passed from initiate to initiate. But it is time for humanity to take more responsibility for its spiritual heritage; work that used to be done by only a select few can now be practiced by many. We have seen this beginning in the last decades as we reconnect with the original wisdom of the First Peoples, and as ancient spiritual practices have come from the East. Times of transition are always dangerous, and maybe some of these practices will be misused. But humanity needs to be given the knowledge that is needed to heal and transform the world.

The simple premise of this book is that there is a vital need to shift our collective culture from a story of separation and exploitation into a new story of living oneness, and that spiritual practice and the love and light it generates have an essential part to play in this shift. Furthermore, spiritual practice can open our hearts to the ancient wisdom of how the Earth functions as a living spiritual being, and together we can work to help heal and regenerate our dying ecosystem, and finally awaken together into a new era. A central aspect of this work is the traditional teaching of the individual being a microcosm of the whole, and just as an individual can spiritually transform and awake, so can the Earth Herself.

I am not suggesting that spiritual activism is the sole form of activism needed to help humanity and the Earth in Her time of distress. There are many ways to bring our hands and hearts into the arena of service, to respond to the "cry of the poor and the cry of the earth." What I am suggesting is that spiritual practice is a little understood catalyst of global change, accessing a power that can help real transformation, a foundational shift that combines the power of the land with the light of our spiritual self. Those who are drawn towards spiritual practice can make a vital contribution to the well-being of the whole.

And a central aspect of spiritual practice is relationship, making a relationship with our own inner light, with the Divine, and with the Earth as a sacred living being. And we live this relationship with our hearts, with love and care and compassion.

This book takes the reader into the arena of spiritual service that belongs to the future. It is not a detailed map or exact description of spiritual practices. This is a time of transition in which the new ways are not yet fully formed. Instead this book outlines some of the foundations, the patterns that are developing in the inner and outer worlds, and the part we have to play in their development. It points to some of the spiritual attitudes we have to leave behind and to others that we should cultivate. It also describes some of the dangers and difficulties of this time of transition, the fault lines of our culture and the vast forces colliding beneath them. Its intent is to expand our perception of what is spiritual life, so that we can respond to the real need of the present time.

At this time little is definite or sure. But just as the Earth cries for our care and compassion, something is coming alive that is changing both us and our planet, and our participation is essential. There is a new story being written, and we are being asked to be present in a new way, to give ourselves in service more completely. These chapters are footsteps to a future that is already present—if we dare to open our eyes. Our Beloved is coming to meet us in a new way, and we are here to open our hearts and say "Yes. Yes. Yes!"

THE FIRST STEP

I saw my Lord in my dreams and I asked,
"How am I to find You?"
He replied, "Leave yourself and come!"

Bâyezîd Bistâmî

Take one step away from yourself and—
Behold—the path.

Abû Sa'îd ibn Abî-l-Khayr

BEYOND SELF-FULFILLMENT

Spiritual energy has tremendous transformative potential. It is a hidden, subtle form of power, known to shamans and spiritual masters throughout time. In the West we have only recently been given direct access to this energy.[1] When spiritual practices and teachings arrived in the West in the last century they brought different forms of working with spiritual energy—meditation, mindfulness, *mantras*, breath practices, sacred dance and music. A generation was awakened to the wonder and power that can be found within, and gradually learned how to use this energy to change their lives. But, as I have mentioned, in this journey to the West one central ingredient to spiritual practice became lost.

The pure energy, light and love of real spiritual energy became subtly covered over by the West's focus on the individual self and what became known as "spiritual materialism." Spiritual energy comes from a direct access to the Divine, from our deepest nature where we are one with God. Like sunlight it is free. But as the different forms of spiritual practice entered the marketplace their focus subtly changed from giving us a simple connection to divine consciousness, light and love, to self-development, health and well-being. The ego, our illusory sense of a separate self, wanted this wonder for itself. And we forgot, or never learned, one of the most basic foundations of all spiritual work, that we should want nothing for ourself, as expressed by the early Sufi saint Râbi'a: "I do not work like a laborer in expectation of wages."

Even in their limited form, these practices and their teachings can bring many positive qualities—presence, a sense of our true nature, more compassion and loving kindness. We can glimpse the unity of life, or "non-duality," and connect with our environment and others in deeper ways. But a quality of spiritual service, of prayer and devotion, does not enter our spectrum of consciousness. Wanting something for ourself we also lose access to a deeper dimension of spiritual energy: how it can nourish and transform not just the individual but also the whole of life. If we are to regain the real potential of this power, if this doorway of real responsibility and service is to open, we need to make sure that we take this "first step"—turning away from ourself. It is both simple and radical, and easily overlooked.

But how can we make this fundamental step when the story that defines our whole culture is that of the individual separate self, that we are separate from each other and separate from the Earth? As with most powerful myths, we have forgotten that this is just a story: even as ecological awareness tells a very different story—that we are part of an interconnected living whole, while science speaks of the interdependence of consciousness and matter. And spiritual teachings tell us that the "I" is the greatest illusion. There is no separate self.

How can we understand this when all we know and are taught to value is the ego? We see our life through the eyes of the ego: our life is about us. This is the face we see in the mirror when we get up in the morning. And at the beginning we can only see the spiritual journey in the framework of the ego and its conditioned values, and so we easily imagine this journey as a process of spiritual self-improvement leading to a deeper and more fulfilling life. Also, as the values of our culture are about self-fulfillment—whether on a material, sexual, or emotional level—we easily project these values onto the spiritual journey. So we merely create a more elevated image of fulfillment. We not only want to be emotionally or sexually fulfilled; we also want "spiritual fulfillment." Into this dream of spiritual fulfillment we may project our unmet needs, images of being self-empowered or finding a meaningful relationship, of being accepted or loved.

As I will explore in the next chapter, such illusions are a natural part of the initial stages of the journey, and should fall away as we get closer to the essential simplicity and emptiness of our true nature. The danger is when self-fulfillment becomes the goal. Then we cannot see beyond the horizon of ourself. And so the spiritual world is contracted into the values of the ego.

But is this all that we can understand? Are we so conditioned by a culture that focuses on self-gratification that we can only be attracted by further images of self-fulfillment? No longer focusing solely on a better material life, we may aspire towards spiritual goals, not realizing that we have just recreated a different form of self-interest, and still remain imprisoned by the ego and its endless cycle of unmet needs. Do we have to remain with these familiar patterns to comfort us? Or are we prepared to acknowledge that this greatest adventure may not be about us?

Our culture both subtly and overtly denies us the teachings and tools that can free us from its self-obsessive grip. We give so much of our lives to its demands of material prosperity that consume our time and energy. Do we also have to surrender our souls to the image of spiritual prosperity? What about the ancient truth that we can experience freedom from the self, and a deeper oneness with life and the Divine? Do we dare to glimpse the vast nature of a journey that can take us far beyond our small self-centered world?

ACCESSING THE POWER OF THE DIVINE

At the present time there is another vital dimension to this question. We are aware that this is a moment of global crisis, that our current collective values, the corporate forces of materialism and greed, are destroying our planet. We may sense that spiritual awareness has an important part to play in healing and transforming our world, and that we have a real responsibility to create change before these forces irrevocably destroy both the outer and inner worlds. But how can we access the spiritual power and potential to create the fundamental change that is needed, when we continue to approach spirituality with the same self-centered values that have created our global predicament?

The very nature of the ego is to see itself as separate: the development of the ego is what creates our sense of a separate self as the child becomes separate from the mother. But the ego also separates us from awareness of the Divine and its all-pervading oneness, which is why as children grow up they only too easily lose contact with life's magical and numinous quality. As we grow older it is our basic identification with the ego that denies us access to our innate spiritual wisdom and power. This is why real spiritual paths teach us to renounce or surrender the ego and why so many present spiritual teachings are subtly corruptive—by promising us the illusion of individual fulfillment, they keep us trapped within the ego and thus deny us access to what is real. If we stay within the values of the ego, we only have access to the energy and vision of the ego, its patterns of illusion. The world cannot be healed by a spiritual illusion based upon the story of separation. But it can be healed by the help of the real power and wisdom of the Divine that is within each of us.

There is a simple truth that is known to all those who commit to spiritual practice. Only the Divine, whether experienced through grace, love, or spiritual power, can really transform us. And what is true for the individual is true for the world. Only the Divine can heal and transform the world—the forces of antagonism in the world are too powerfully constellated for us to resolve on our own; the patterns of greed and exploitation that are draining the lifeblood of the planet and destroying its ecosystem are too firmly entrenched. But we cannot fully have access to the energy of the Divine unless we step beyond our ego-self.

The power of the Divine can be understood in many different ways. It is the light of the Self—our soul or divine nature, the sacred forces in creation, the real joy of life, the energy of our true nature, God's love. True spiritual traditions that look beyond the ego connect us with this power, and then teach us how to bring it into life: how to live from the divine center of ourself in the midst of everyday life. They teach us how to be of service to the Divine and not to the desires of the ego. These spiritual traditions also teach that sacrifice is part of the journey. In Sufism we are taught to "die before we die"; to surrender the values of the ego in order to embrace the larger dimension of the soul. Without this attitude of surrender or sacrifice there can be no real journey, nor can we live a life of true service.

With the correct attitude of surrender and spiritual service we can go beyond the ego and its limitations, and step into the dimension of our divine nature, the Self. In order to bring this quality into life, the Divine needs our participation. We need to work with the power of love for the well-being of the whole.

Our ego-oriented life has created a fragmented world of conflict, with different factions striving for dominance. We have to compete and struggle, caught in the images of winners and losers and all of the other dramas of dualism. In this world, we have to look out for ourself because no one else will. In our separateness we also often feel alone and isolated, impotent to effect real change. Moreover, it is partly due to our self-created illusion of being separate from the Earth that we are destroying its fragile web. If we realized how intrinsically we are interconnected with the Earth, we would never treat it just as a resource to be exploited.

Once we step outside of the illusion of our own separate self, a radically different picture emerges. Our true nature exists in a dimension of oneness. Unlike the ego, which always looks out for its own self-interest, the Self reflects a vision of unity, in which each individual part is nourished according to its real need. A glimpse of the Self gives us a sense of an interconnected oneness in which nothing is separate: everything is an expression of a oneness that is dynamically alive. Every person, every stone, is this oneness; everything is connected and interdependent. Our individual Self is the Universal Self and it is all a living organism of light and love.

When we live with a conscious awareness of our intrinsic oneness, we bring this oneness into our culture's collective consciousness, which is dying through the illusion of separation. Our light *is* the light of the world; our divine consciousness *is* the spiritual consciousness of the world—nothing is separate. When we turn away from the ego and its desires, we know that we embody this sacred substance. And we are also life, hungry for what is sacred. In the dynamic interconnected whole, we are the in-breath and out-breath of life—a life that is not just physical existence, but a multidimensional living organism of light and love. We are the spiritual lifeblood of the planet and we need to honor this dimension of life, this quality of oneness that is present within everything, and can be felt within our own heart.

GLOBAL ONENESS AND SELF-INTEREST

We need the power of the Divine with its vision of oneness in order to step from the story of separation into an understanding of global wholeness. Through the eyes of love we discover that we are part of an interdependent physical and spiritual ecosystem in which each part nourishes and supports the whole. Our survival and evolution will depend upon our understanding the interrelationships between the parts and how they dynamically work together. The heart contains the seeds of this understanding because it always sees everything as a reflection of the whole. Our divine nature *is* the oneness of the world, which is also the oneness of God. Through a creative relationship with our higher nature we can bring an understanding of oneness into our lives, learn to live according to its principles and knowledge. We can live the story of divine love told in the pages of our daily life.

Oneness is not an abstract idea but a living expression of the true nature of life and the Earth. The oneness of all of life is a manifestation of the divine oneness that is within our own heart and soul. And just as humanity has been given and also developed a body of knowledge of how to work with our inner divine nature—practices to help transform ourself and realize our higher consciousness—we are also being given access now to a knowledge of how oneness works in the world. It is essential that we rediscover this higher knowledge of life, so that life itself can be transformed. We have separated matter and spirit and denied the sacred nature of all of creation for too long. Through the power of this collective forgetfulness we have starved the Earth. Collectively we no longer pray for the Earth in our daily rituals, rarely practice praise and thanksgiving. We now need to return the potency of the spirit to the Earth and understand how this living being really functions. We need to regain an understanding of the spiritual principles that underlie creation and how to work with these principles.

This knowledge of the sacred nature of creation is waiting to be accessed. It is present within the spiritual body of the Earth, just as our own higher wisdom is present in our higher consciousness. But this knowledge cannot be accessed by a consciousness that is focused on the ego. It will only reveal itself to a consciousness that looks to the well-being of the whole. Sadly, because so much contemporary spiritual teaching focuses solely on our individual spiritual well-being, many people do not even know that it exists. That is why it is essential that we take the first step and recognize how we limit and isolate ourselves. In the words of the Sufi martyr al-Hallâj, "The first step is to cease isolating ourself from God."

Divine wholeness is waiting to be lived. It includes every cell of creation, the wisdom within every plant and animal, the flow of the tides and the movement of the stars. It is a deep instinctual knowing about how the world works as a living, breathing, spiritual being. And it is very practical. This is not an idealistic spiritual theory but a knowing that belongs to the basic principles of life: everything is sacred and can live in harmony and balance. In this balance the real needs of life are met, even though many of our self-induced desires and addictions will have to be sacrificed. The world is not here to give us what we want: the world is an expression of divine love that needs us to help it to realize its full potential.

We need to regain the wisdom of previous cultures that understood that we are here to work together with the sacred within life. We have been given the responsibility to help creation to evolve, to be co-creators in the deepest sense. Recognizing this spiritual and ecological responsibility belongs to the next step in our collective evolution. It is partly in order to learn this that we have constellated such a precipitous global situation. Only when we take real responsibility for the Earth can we avert our present ecological disaster.

This is a major shift that humanity has to make, and the global dimension of our present problems—the crisis of climate change, the toxicity of our air and oceans— points to the need to shift into a global awareness. And yet the forces that resist any real change have drawn us into fear and isolationism. This is the real battle that is being fought. We vitally need the knowledge of oneness, but the patterns that deny us this knowledge are being reinforced. Global communication, the internet, and social media connect us throughout the world. But collectively we seem unable to step beyond our self-interest and embrace the oneness of life and the world. Of course there is a price for this step. In the West we will have to lose many of the privileges we have taken for ourselves. We might have to sacrifice our dominance and the greed we disguise as consumerism.

THE SPIRITUAL PRINCIPLES WITHIN LIFE

The higher principles within life are waiting to be discovered and used. As a living spiritual being, the Earth can function in ways that are hidden to us at present. When we see the world through the prism of our self-centered material consciousness, we are unaware of its real nature and potential. The work of those who have been given the gift and responsibility of a spiritual awareness is to become attuned to the higher potential of life. Spiritual seekers have always been pioneers, going beyond the surface values of the collective to explore a deeper reality. We have sensed or experienced dimensions within ourself that are beyond the physical, and our dreams and visions have told us how these dimensions can transform our life. Now we need to bring this awareness into the arena of global oneness, to step aside from focusing on our individual development and recognize this larger stage. Just as there is hidden knowledge and spiritual potential within each of us, there are similar qualities within the spiritual body of the Earth, and it is for us to discover them—to be receptive to their unveiling.

The world is not going to be saved by politicians or corporations, but by those in service to the real need of both humanity and the Earth—those who truly "care for our common home." Higher knowledge has always come from within, but it needs those committed to this revelation to bring it into life, to unite the inner and outer and help awaken the world to its spiritual nature. Our eyes can see the plight of our world, the problems we have created. Our hearts and higher consciousness can be attuned to divine oneness and the harmony and peace that are within. Bringing together these different levels of awareness enables the inner to influence the outer.

During the past era our focus has been on a transcendent, often disembodied spirituality. As a result we have forgotten the very practical nature of our true self. In the dimension of oneness everything is included. There is nothing higher or lower, nothing that is not sacred. Spiritual knowledge belongs to the whole of life, to each cell of creation. The soul is present within the whole body of each of us and also within the body of the Earth. Spiritual principles offer us a very practical way to work with the energies of life.

Our culture, based upon science and technology, may appear to present us with a tangible, definable world divorced from the vagaries of the spirit. But we have forgotten that the father of our Western culture— Parmenides, the man who invented logic, the basis of our reasoning—was a mystic who received his teaching from the Goddess.[2] Spirituality is a science of how things really are. It helps us to understand the essence of things. A spiritual understanding attunes us not only to the real meaning of our life, but also to how life comes into existence and to the forces behind creation. A transcendent divinity may require abstract metaphysics, but once we return the Divine to its rightful place within creation, spirituality becomes something very different: a practical way to work with the sacred energy that is within creation, a way to use this energy to benefit all of life. But before we can have access to this spiritual knowledge we have to develop the correct receptive attitude. We need to expand our spiritual consciousness from our own inner journey into the greater wholeness of life's unfolding. We can achieve this realization at the end of the inner journey, when we discover that our individual Self *is* the Universal Self. Or we can make this shift through a simple expansion of consciousness that acknowledges the global dimension to oneness: we are a part of the whole of life. Nothing is separate. What is within us is within the world. Within our spiritual consciousness are the secrets not only of our own awakening but of the awakening of the planet.

When we have an attitude of consciousness that is receptive to this dimension of spirituality, we can have access to the knowledge that belongs to life's unfolding. This knowledge is waiting to be given to humanity. The world needs our help in order to evolve. This new knowledge will cover the spectrum of our lives, from new ways of healing to the use of the non-polluting energy of sunlight as a basic power source. We will learn how the principles of oneness can take goods and materials where they are really needed around the world, serving rather than exploiting, and adapt our financial institutions to this new organic model. We have seen with the rapid development of the internet how such new technologies are efficient and cost-effective in ways that we could not have imagined.

Esoteric knowledge that belongs to the spiritual awakening of the Earth will also be available to us. Without this inner core of spiritual teachings all the other developments will only function on the surface and at a fraction of their real potential. The awakening of the spiritual body of the Earth will enable us to understand life in a completely new way, founded upon oneness rather than separation. It will give us access to power sources within the Earth that are needed for our development. And as the world comes alive, humanity and the planet will interrelate in a completely new way.

According to ancient tradition, the individual is a microcosm of the whole of creation (in Sufism "the lesser adam in relation to the greater Adam"). Similarly the spiritual body of the Earth is a macrocosm of the spiritual body of the individual and follows similar ways of awakening. It cannot be forced but requires an understanding of the energies within the world and within the individual and of how they interrelate and resonate with each other. This belongs to a new level of spiritual awareness that will be given to humanity. Each era of the world and humanity's evolution requires a new body of spiritual knowledge, and as Christ said at the beginning of the last era:

> And no man putteth new wine into old bottles: else the new wine doth burst the bottles, and the wine is spilled, and the bottles will be marred: but new wine must be put into new bottles.[3]

This means that each era requires a new attitude to contain the spiritual teachings that are becoming accessible. That is why the first step is to leave behind our present conditioning that focuses on our individual self. Only then can we be receptive to this new dimension of spiritual understanding.

SPIRITUAL MATURITY
AND SERVICE

When it is time for stillness, stillness;
in the time of companionship, companionship;
at the place of effort, effort.
Everything at its time and its place.

Naqshbandi Saying

Around us is an unending revelation. In every instant
the Divine is being born anew. And yet at this moment
in our history we are also at the beginning of a new era;
a new pattern of life is coming into being. Our spiritual
awareness is central to this birth. In our hearts, in our
consciousness, and with every breath, we are midwives to
a new awakening of the Earth that is taking place now. In
order to participate fully in this birth, we have to leave
behind old patterns, old ways of walking on the earth
and of looking towards heaven. We are stepping into an
era of oneness that will bring together matter and spirit,
feminine and masculine, and our spiritual practice must
reflect this new alignment. We cannot renounce the
Earth or follow a patriarchal model of spiritual progress.
Our soul's journey is part of the journey of the whole of
creation. Our heart is connected to the heart of the world.
Our remembrance is the remembrance of the Earth. Our
awakening can help the world to awaken.

And yet the individual journey back to the Source, the lover back to the Beloved, continues as it always has. Everything changes and nothing changes. The journey Home is like the spiritual heartbeat of the world. When a seeker turns towards the Beloved, all of creation rejoices, because this is the innermost song for all of life. Every atom longs to be reunited with its Beloved, and as spiritual wayfarers we live this longing with our whole being. This journey is our greatest contribution to life and to our Beloved. We offer ourselves on the altar of divine love and live the primal drama of separation and union.

As we expand our spiritual consciousness to include the whole of creation, it is important to remember the simplicity and ordinariness of the soul's journey and how it is lived in everyday life. The heart's longing for God belongs to the primal essence of life. Just as a sunflower follows the Sun, so does our soul look to its Source. To live and breathe this true calling often means having to leave behind many of the images that we may have about spiritual life. And if we are to reconnect our own journey with life's journey, we have to be especially careful—to walk the path as mature adults, not just creating a different level of illusion.

Just as we need to take the first step away from ourself in order to access the deeper dimension of spiritual energy, we need to learn spiritual maturity if we are to be of real service to life and the Divine.

THE INNOCENCE OF AWAKENING

At the beginning of the journey a spark of pure love touches our heart and we awake for an instant to the wonder of our real nature and our innermost union with

God. Without this gift of love there would be no journey, no desire to turn towards God. We would remain within the clouds of forgetfulness, never knowing our true self. This spark brings us alive and turns our attention towards the journey of the soul, the greatest adventure.

Traditionally called "the turning of the heart," this awakening of love is like a first romance, except that this is no idealized lover, no romantic fantasy; this is the great love affair of the soul with God, bursting into consciousness. And yet it often evokes in the lover a similar quality of adolescent impetuousness, creating spiritual fantasies that, like their romantic counterparts, often spin out of control. It is not always easy to reconcile this awakening to real love with the mundanities of our everyday life, or to contain this innermost desire within our ordinary consciousness.

This turning of the heart awakens a spark within us. Ultimately this becomes the fire that will burn and consume us, transform our lead into gold. But at the beginning it is just a crazy passion that has no container. We may identify it as "longing for God," but we have no notion of the real dynamics of the journey, the painful work upon the shadow and lower self, the slow grinding down of the ego that belong to the initial years of the quest. Just as the romantic experience of falling in love does not prepare us for the real work of a relationship, the spark that touches us in the heart of hearts does not make us think of the vast and dangerous nature of what is happening. We are thrown into the divine love affair as a blind person into an infinite ocean.

This is the way it has always been. We come with innocence and longing, confused by doubts and insecurities, filled with a desire for something we cannot understand. Nor do we know what to do with the intensity and passion of the soul. What can we do except create spiritual fantasies, images of some spiritual world filled with what is unfulfilled within us?

Maybe the journey will give us the partner we have always wanted, the work we feel we deserve. We so easily project our personal needs onto the unknown potential of the quest, looking for a parent to love us, a lover to embrace us, friends to understand us, work to fulfill us. In the West this natural tendency towards projection is augmented by a conditioning that promotes instant gratification and tells us we have the right to personal happiness. The long hard road of real spiritual life has little place in our collective consciousness.

The difficulty is compounded by the fact that at the beginning we are shown something that is immediate, belonging to the eternal Now. We are given a glimpse of what is here always, our eternal Beloved. There is no time in this moment, no long and arduous journey. Instead there is something spontaneously and completely alive. We are seduced by being given a taste of what is already within us—the gift of ourselves as we eternally are. How can the ego with its restrictions in time and space understand or live this eternal Now?

The wayfarer does not initially understand that the real work on the path is not to have access to spiritual or mystical experiences; these are given through grace. The work is to create a container for them, so they can come alive in our daily life. So we can learn to live the deepest desire of the heart without being caught in unnecessary illusions and distractions. Without the container of a grounded life and real discrimination the wayfarer easily becomes lost and wastes the energy and potential of her awakening.

SPIRITUAL ILLUSIONS

This does not mean one should dismiss the excitement and fire of one's awakening. Traditionally this is one's spiritual rebirth, the moment the real life of the soul begins. The "Yes" that until now has been hidden within the soul comes to the surface, sometimes exploding into our outer world. There are a joy and an intensity that belong to this moment, that need to be lived. Real love has arrived; real light is present. Something tremendous has begun. There can be a sense of "coming home," for the first time in one's life, of being where one truly belongs. Every phase of the path has its place, "there is a time for everything under the sun."

I remember the intensity of my own awakening, the world suddenly sparkling with a hidden light, the joy and wonder of it all. I remember my first experiences in meditation, my first experiences of an inner reality beyond the mind. I was given something I had always longed for but did not know existed. I was given a taste of what is real in the midst of a world of illusions and lies. The desire for Truth was ignited and I knew what I wanted. I had no container for the crazy passion that possessed me: it drove me almost to madness; I fasted beyond what my body could bear. But for the first time I was completely alive.

Hopefully one finds a teacher or a path to begin the work of creating a container, of channeling the fire in the right direction, so that one can live a balanced life. It was three years before I found the path that would take me Home, and I arrived there in a state far from balanced, hanging on through will and determination, thin, hungry, and with my feet hardly touching the ground. But we are each given the experiences we need, and I do not regret the craziness of those initial years, even though I know

now that much of my energy and most of my actions were misplaced. I remember living off bowls of brown rice, sitting, staring at a wall with an empty mind for days, hoping to emerge into a higher consciousness. I still remember the blue-colored wall of the room where I sat, but little more. I had to realize that one cannot fast the body into perfection, or reach reality by force of will.

One of the dangers of the early years is spiritual illusions. We are gripped by a longing, a primal hunger for something we cannot name and do not know. We are awakened for an instant to a reality that has little echo in our outer life or inner thought-patterns. We have no context for what is actually taking place, and so naturally we create images and expectations of the path. The moment I saw the light in my teacher's eyes, I wanted to be in that space beyond the limitations of a world that I found increasingly alienating and problem-filled. I imagined that spiritual life was to live in that formless dimension of presence and love. I little imagined how the path would force me back into this world of limitations, how family life and being in service to others would be my greatest teachers.

Many seekers fall into this illusion of escape from ordinary reality at the beginning of the journey. As one friend describes it, "I thought that I would be taken out of life. That ordinary, outer life would fade away somehow, that I wouldn't have to be responsible in life. I thought I would be lost in love. That I wouldn't have to exist as a 'separate' individual any more, that I would always be swept away in love. I thought I would be taken deeper and deeper into states of love and bliss. That it would be like going farther and farther into meditation. I really didn't think I would ever have to come back into normal life, or normal awareness."

Another friend thought that her problems would no longer exist, that they would fade away or she would rise above them to exist in a higher reality. Other seekers create the illusion that they will acquire special spiritual knowledge, or even spiritual powers. The promise of "enlightenment" is a common delusion, one that overlooks the basic truth that the ego does not have any higher experiences and that in the dimension of the Self there is no "I" to realize anything. So many illusions, so many ways we use images of the path as a way to escape from life and from ourselves. The real path takes us back to ourselves and into life. If we do not come back into ourselves, the important grounding psychological work—the confrontation with our own darkness, the shadow, and other inner dynamics that help create the container of a balanced psyche—would never be done.

As we work upon ourself, we begin to see that many of the initial illusions of the path have to do with our experience of the ego as the sole actor in our life. One friend understood that her illusions "are all born from the obvious fact that a 'person' comes to the path, so everything I initially expected referred back to the 'personal.' For example, I thought 'I' or the 'personal self' would be in love all the time. I didn't realize that love just *is*. That it has nothing really to do with 'me,' but it just exists."

As I have mentioned, at the beginning all that we know is the "I," and so we imagine the path and its experiences through the eyes of the ego, with all its desires and images of fulfillment. Even if we have read or been told that the ego "has to go," that the path is a process of annihilation, we cannot imagine a state in which the "I" is not at the center. When we think of the Self, we imagine a spiritualized ego. We are rarely prepared for the simplicity of what *is*. The Self may have a cosmic dimension, but it is also the most ordinary and simple essence, a quality of being that is present in everything. To live this essential simplicity of self is one of the real tests of the path.

While some illusions center on an inner spiritual state, others reflect a desire to manifest something in the outer, for example becoming a healer or even a spiritual teacher, having a "destiny" that we think reflects our unique spiritual nature. While some wayfarers may be called down these paths, the wish for them is often just a new form of ego-gratification, in which the ego gets hold of a pure energy or intention and uses it for its own purposes. The ego loves to make itself special, the central actor on every stage. It can be disillusioning to realize that the Self often does not need any specific outer form or role to manifest, that it is a state of being rather than a "manifest destiny."

Often the illusions of the path are an avoidance of real responsibility for our life and actions. It is a perfect excuse for someone who does not want to fully embrace everyday life with its difficulties and demands. Patriarchal spirituality may have stressed the transcendent nature of the Self, but the Self is also an intrinsic part of life, and it can only be fully incarnated and lived when we take full responsibility for life as it is. One can only realize the Self with the full acceptance of one's life. In the words of the Sufi master Abû Sa'îd ibn Abî-l-Khayr, "Whatever is to be your fate, face it!"

Finally, the path takes us to a place where the ego surrenders and the Self becomes the ruler. Then life takes on the quality of a blank sheet of paper for true spiritual service. But by the time we have reached this stage, we have taken full responsibility for our life, for the ego and its needs and demands. We have become mature wayfarers who do not use the path to avoid life's difficulties. We have learned the value of common sense, and learned how to live in both worlds. And we have developed constant vigilance against the ego and its cunning ways of self-deception.

ORDINARY LIFE

Perhaps no illusion is more common or more insidious than the illusion that spiritual life will take the seeker away from ordinary life. Ordinary life will always be included. In fact, we become more and more immersed in the ordinary: we "chop wood and carry water."

Often it is the mundanity of the path for which we are least prepared. After a taste of the passion of the soul, which initially seems so "other" to our common experience, we tend to expect the banality of life to fade away in the excitement or ecstasy of the inner journey. We may imagine a spiritual life filled with dramatic challenges and spiritual states. But that is simply the ego yet again co-opting the experience for its own ends. Just to be an ordinary wayfarer walking a dusty path Home is not so gratifying.

The true uniqueness of our nature often appears most ordinary and simple. As one friend describes her experience, "I am always shocked by how ordinary things are, how I keep coming *down* into the ordinary. I really expected things to seem extra-ordinary." Another friend who came to be with my teacher expected to live a simple life of meditation, but within a few years she found herself teaching in an inner-city primary school, with thirty children demanding her attention all day long. It was not what she imagined!

Often the attachment to the "extra-ordinariness" of spiritual life is another way to protect ourselves from life, or from ourself, just as a romantic fantasy can protect us from the vulnerability and demands of a real relationship. True love makes us naked and vulnerable, as the patterns that protect us are dissolved or burned away. Unlike most illusions, the real nature of the path is about becoming emptier, having less rather than more. While illusions often inflate the ego with images of being special, on the real path we become more ordinary and simple.

When we feel we are living the passion of the soul, torn apart by love, we can easily dismiss the importance of paying our bills on time, of taking care of our human needs and responsibilities. We can go through life with little attention to how we treat others, and how we treat ourselves. But without a firm ground in the ordinary, without learning how to relate to life with the attention and respect it needs—care and loving kindness for those around us—we cannot fully live the energy of the soul *here*.

A focus on ordinary life grounds the energy of the path, and also makes it more difficult for the ego to create spiritual fantasies. This is why traditionally when a young man first came to a Sufi *tekke*, or *khânqâh* (Turkish and Persian for "Sufi center or hospice"), he was given the most mundane or debasing tasks, for example cleaning the latrines, sweeping the courtyard. For the first few years he might be given no spiritual practices at all, only simple tasks of service.

It is important to not reject the ordinary dimension of our experience, because the nature of the soul is ordinary and simple, and often expresses itself in what is most ordinary. The soul is a quality of being in which things just *are*. Here peace *is*, love *is*, even power just *is*. We will never notice, let alone really live, these qualities of the soul if we follow our desires to escape the ordinary, if we create unnecessary dramas or fantasies. Zen *haiku* often reflect this simplicity. The dew on the grass is present in the moment without any drama. The full Harvest Moon on the water is both simple and profound. The container we are creating on the path is a mature relationship with life. We will never be able to live the paradox of how the ordinary and extraordinary come together if we are not willing to accept life as it is.

The real work is to stay true to ourself with all the demands of everyday life, to keep the inner attention, even for five minutes a day, when there are so many distractions. Remembrance is no longer performed in seclusion, but in the office and the supermarket. The path may be the opposite of what we expect; it may be paradoxical, confusing, and contrary to our conditioning, but it needs to be lived in this world, to be part of everyday life.

And at this particular stage in the evolution of humanity, the ordinariness of life has a new meaning. In the era now dawning, it will be able to reflect the numinosity of the soul in a new way. But in order to allow life to reflect the richness and eternal nature of the soul, we must let go of patterns both personal and collective that turn us away from the ordinary. We need to learn to discriminate between a Disneyland fantasy of spiritual life, full of roller-coaster rides and cotton candy, and the real way the Divine is present in the world around us.

FROM INNOCENCE TO EXPERIENCE

And now that life is calling for us to participate spiritually in its unfolding, it is vital that we are not just caught in further illusions. We are neither hero nor saint. We are not here to save the world but to engage creatively in life *as it is*, to pray for the Earth as we would a sick parent or lover. Illusions just cover over our light, distort our perception, give voice to the ego and its song of separation. To face the world as it is today, with clear eyes and compassion, requires real maturity. We have to see the darkness of our present time and its effects on our beloved Earth, and also recognize how this darkness seeps into our own souls. We feel the grief of how we are polluting the land, the water, the air, and at the loss of species, the clear-cut forests. And in the midst of this darkening world, we need to stay true to our own light and our love for the Earth.

Love's revolution began with a spark of love and oneness in the mid-1960s. We were all children, dreaming of a future other than the grey world of materialism. We sang and danced, loved and meditated, welcoming in a new era with an innocence that was bound to crash into the harsh light of reality. Yes, the seeds of love's oneness were sown, but like every young lover we were full of illusions, and while some seeds grew into environmental consciousness, spiritual communities, holistic health, we mainly lacked the maturity and wisdom of how to water and tend these seeds over the decades.

The world's distractions claimed the attention of many of us, the ten thousand things which so quickly became ten million things. As I have mentioned, many practices became distorted, as well as spiritual teachers becoming corrupted. The light was not lost, just covered over, and the seeds remained mostly underground. And now we face a future more bleak than we could have imagined. Seeing the divisive world around us, the pain of the Earth on which we walk, the road of return to love, oneness, and wonder looks hard and stony.

But this is traditionally the way the journey unfolds. In the Grail legend of the wounded Fisher King, when the naïve and innocent young Sir Parsifal found himself in the grounds of the Grail Castle it was a wondrous, unexpected, unearned gift. But then it disappeared, and he had to struggle on the lonely pathways of the world for years, filled with trials and quests, before the Grail Castle returned. By then he was mature and experienced enough to remain with the Grail and the work of healing the King that was required.

And now, half a century after that first love song, are we mature enough to do the real work of bringing our light into life, our heart to healing the Earth? Can we be grounded in our awareness of oneness, in our desire to live the primal unity of all of creation? Can we be practical in the challenges facing us? Or will we just create another illusion, another dream to escape a world whose wounds we dare not really face?

PATIENCE AND THE PATTERNS OF CHANGE

Hopefully having faced the illusions of our own individual journey, having confronted our own darkness, we no longer look for an escape either from ourselves or the ordinary in daily life. We have found a grounded simplicity that also includes love and care for others. Innocence has matured into experience, and we are ready to make a real spiritual contribution to life, to nourish the seeds of love and work to heal our wounded Earth.

And during our journey we should have developed qualities to help us: compassion and loving kindness towards others, a sense of the sacred, a clearer inner light to guide us. Common sense and a sense of humor balance us, integrity keeps us from being caught in life's present toxicity. And especially important for this stage of the work are perseverance and patience.

One of the reasons that we need to learn patience on the inner journey is that we are working with the rhythms of the soul, rather than the time scale of the ego. Rûmî expresses this with simple beauty:

> Love, the new moon, grows slowly stage by stage;
> We should progress like that, deliberately, with
>   patience....
> God perfected his clay by slow, perfect degrees.
> Not like you, crazy one, rushing everything always.[1]

The inner processes of the soul develop slowly, maturing like wine. They belong to the eternal dimension of ourself, not the hectic, stress-filled rush of our days. In Sufism travelling the stages of the path takes between twenty to thirty years, if one remains attentive and committed. And the evolution of the World Soul belongs to the rhythm of millennia, each era of humanity taking two thousand years. As our present time appears to hurry forward second by second, we have lost touch with the deeper flow of time, with the passing of life's seasons, and have no understanding of cosmic time. Unlike, for example, the Mayan civilization whose Long Count Calendar—which ended on 21st December 2012 and was much hyped and misunderstood—reflected a galactic realignment that might not impact our consciousness for centuries.

If we are to work together with these seasons of the sacred, we need to learn to wait—attentive, watching, but profoundly patient. In the Indigenous traditions there was an understanding of this, as for example in the Iroquois philosophy that the decisions we make today should result in a sustainable world seven generations into the future. Yes, we are at a time of profound change, but it is a change that has been constellating for centuries. It can be said that our climate change crisis began with the industrial revolution and the industrial scale use of coal.[2]

While the shift into a story of oneness, of interbeing, may have been ignited in the summer of love, its origins can be traced to the violent repression of paganism and earth-based spirituality in the early years of Christianity.[3] For how long could we deny our relationship to the sacred nature of creation? Today's vital need to reconnect with the sacred within the Earth and within our own bodies began centuries ago.

And now, as we watch the Earth dying, there is an urgency. The climate change crisis points to the disaster of two degrees or more warming. But the work of those who "keep watch on the world and for the world" is to stay attuned to the deeper rhythms of the Soul of the World and its patterns of evolution. Just as we are trained not to get caught in the illusions of our present time, we need to be mature enough in our practice not to be caught in panic. We are working with a shift that stretches across millennia, and it cannot be forced. Yes, as Thich Nhat Hanh said, there are "bells of mindfulness" in our ecological crisis, and prompt action is needed in many areas—carbon emissions, dramatically reducing our use of plastic for example—but their sound should also remind us of the dangers of a lack of real attention. There is no "quick fix," but rather a deep rebalancing is needed. Otherwise, like our attempts at "greening the economy," we will avoid the deeper patterns at play, and continue our fantasies for a future that continues to darken, just with a different form of economic exploitation, a different dance of separation.

Spiritual maturity means to live in the moment, mindful, aware, without being caught in the immediacy of action and reaction that appears to govern so much of today's world, with its short attention span and continual news cycles. We are trained to respond to the real need of the moment while we stay attentive to what is beneath the surface. When I compiled a book of essays describing the inner landscape of this present time, I titled it *Darkening of the Light*,[4] not just to refer to the present loss of the light of the sacred, but also to relate to hexagram thirty-six of the *I Ching*, or *Book of Changes*:

> The light has sunk into the earth:
> The image of Darkening of the Light.

The Taoist masters understood the patterns of change that belong to the underlying flow of life, and it is these patterns, this flow of life, that need our care and attention. It is here that the future is constellated into form. Alarm bells may be ringing, but unless we work to help life change from deep within, nothing new can be born.

COLLIDING FORCES

And now we stare astonished at the sea,
And a miraculous strange bird shrieks at us.

W. B. Yeats[1]

THE FAULT LINE

Collectively we are walking along a fault line. There are vast pressures building up under our feet, primal powers in the depths which have been moving for centuries. We feel tensions in the air around us, the threat to the ecosystem, the conflicts of terrorism. But within the ground, greater forces are building, forces that belong to the future and not the present. Mostly we walk unknowingly, sensing something but having little knowledge of these vaster forces that are shaping our collective destiny.

The fault line on which we are walking is the place where two eras meet. When one era ends and another begins, forces of a whole different magnitude collide. Because these energies move so slowly, constellating over centuries, we do not recognize the enormous scale of what is taking place.

A physical earthquake occurs when two geological plates collide. The fault line is where the plates meet and the pressure erupts, breaking through the fragile surface of the Earth that up to that moment seemed so immovable.

A different earthquake could come as the forces of the inner world break through the surface structures of our lives. The inner forces of our individual and collective unconscious are as powerful and as hidden as the physical forces that create continents. In our personal psyche they can break through into our conscious self, triggered by an event, causing an emotional or psychological crisis. Sometimes they erupt in the collective psyche in wars and migrations, shaping our collective destiny. They can cause immense suffering, as in the recent civil wars in South Sudan and Syria; or bring freedom, as in the sudden fall of the Berlin Wall and the end of communism in Europe, or the Arab Spring—though this was sadly followed by violent government repression and conflict, leading to what has been called the Arab Winter.

What will happen when such an earthquake comes? How will we respond? We know that our present patterns of response are inadequate. We have experienced our reactions to the disturbances in our world: how we contract around our fear and cling to our possessions in order to protect our "way of life." How we project our fears onto "the other." The global crisis of climate change and environmental collapse, despite its vast implications, for many evokes a strange apathy, a collective denial. Even the term "sustainability" now refers to sustaining our present energy-intensive materialistic culture, rather than real sustainability for all of life.

But what if the very earth that we stand on, on which we have built our lives, begins to move? Will we be able to find more adequate, more productive ways of responding? Many talk of a new story, a new era of global consciousness. But few understand the magnitude and power of the changes taking place. Mostly we notice the surface changes—increased economic and political divisiveness, fear of terrorism or refugees, the spread of fake news. But these are just symptoms of something deeper, like the changing patterns of birds in flight before a storm. In fact there are real signs around us, but they are written in a language we mostly have forgotten. And we cannot imagine what they are telling us, because the shifts that are taking place have not happened for so long that we do not have the images in our collective memory, except in myths of when the gods walked among us. Sometimes a poet may glimpse a truth and use his craft to translate the signs, as Yeats did when he wrote,

> Turning and turning in the widening gyre
> The falcon cannot hear the falconer;
> Things fall apart; the center cannot hold....
>
> Surely some revelation is at hand;
> Surely the Second Coming is at hand....
> And what rough beast, its hour come round at last,
> Slouches towards Bethlehem to be born?[2]

Yeats sensed that something was falling apart and something was waiting to be born. But he had only the images of the past to translate his vision. And the past is not what is happening. What is falling apart is the very fabric of our civilization, but what is to be born comes from the core of creation, from a new dimension of being. That is why we find it so difficult to read the signs that are all around us. We can feel the pressure that is building, the fault line in the midst of our consumer culture. But we have lived on the surface of life for so long that we have no sense of the real intensity of power that is building up beneath the surface, and no knowledge of the purpose of this power.

SIMPLE ANSWERS

When one era ends and another begins, power is generated to bring the new era into being. The power is needed to help dissolve the images and structures of the past, to destroy what is old and help the new to be born. Collectively, we must let go of many patterns and ways of relating if we are to embrace an entirely new way of being and living together. For example, we will have to move beyond the sense of security we have tied to material prosperity. Attachments around money, material goods, and property will have to give way to a deeper source of safety and well-being if we are to move with the changes that are coming.

Our outdated patterns are already losing their value for us. Many sense this, and are feeling a deep anxiety around issues of security, around fear of not being in control. But are we looking closely at the source of this anxiety? Do we recognize the changes that are possible? Are we allowing the old to fall apart, to reveal the new?

Despite deep fears of economic instability, terrorism, or being overrun by migrants, the anxiety that is present in our culture does not come from any outside force. We fear that we are losing our way of life, and in that we are correct. But not in the way we understand or react to. The danger of climate change is real, but in the depths of our psyche we are sensing that something in our foundation no longer holds. This is the deep reason for our collective unease, which we project onto outer forces that appear to threaten us.

It is time to look closely at what is really happening. The mystic and spiritual practitioner has always known that in order to find the cause of any effect we have to turn our attention inward—to look at the inner patterns.

We look to the hints in our dreams; we read the images of our psyche that are not censored by our conscious conditioning. When Joseph interpreted the dreams of the seven years of plenty and the seven lean years, Egypt was saved from a catastrophe.

And yet we have rejected the images of the inner as belonging to a mythological past or the psychiatrist's couch. Instead, we listen to the voices of the outer experts. But with so many newscasters, political and economic analysts, and even spiritual teachers, how do we know whom and what to trust? And do we even know how to listen?

If we look carefully, we can find a thread that links it all together—links our dreams and the stories on the news, links the trivial, the mundane, and the sensational. There is a thread that is our collective destiny, and it is inside each of us, as well as in the world around us.

This thread is so simple it is overlooked. It is so ordinary we pass it by. It is in our hope, in our need to be loved, in the warmth of a handshake or the touch of a kiss. It can be found in empathy, the most basic connection between human beings, not the words we say but in feelings and the very nature of communication. It is in the simple fact that we all live together on this planet—the primal knowing that we are one.

NEW CONNECTIONS

Because we live at the end of an era, life has apparently become more complex. This is one of the signs of things falling apart. With our computer-generated models we look for complex answers to our problems.

The signs of the emerging culture are not complex. They are in patterns that unify, that bring things together, rather than destroy and break things into myriad pieces. The danger arises when we turn away from what is offered, through either ignorance or arrogance—when we stick to our models of ever-increasing complexity rather than recognize the simple human values that belong to our being.

We do not have to save or protect our culture. We do not have the power to resist the dynamics of change, even though we are collectively experiencing many forces of regression. Nor do we have to create a new culture. We have neither the energy nor the knowledge for such an undertaking.

But we do have a responsibility: to listen, to love and be loved, and to become aware of what is really happening. We have to accept that *we* cannot save the Earth, just as we cannot defeat the forces of corruption. Enough battles have been fought, and the Earth is a living being that can heal itself, with our love and cooperation.

What we always seem to overlook is the simple wonder of being human, which means to be divine. We are the meeting of the two worlds, the place where miracles can happen and the Divine come alive in a new way. We are the light at the end of the tunnel. We are the warmth and the care and the compassion, as much as we carry the scars of our cruelty and anger.

This coming change is so fundamental—it is a return to what is simple and essential, what is basic to life. And yet it is not easy to live. Many forces push us outwards towards complexity. These are the forces that take away our joy and demand that we work harder and harder. They drive us into conflicts we do not need and always try to obscure the simple joy of life, of being together and valuing our companionship. Fast food and mega-movies may glitter and catch our collective attention, but we know in our hearts that something fundamental is being overlooked. We do not need to drown in prosperity. Nor do we need to impose any beliefs on others. We have simply to recognize what is *real* and live this in our own lives. What is real has the energy and light to free us from so many imposed beliefs. If we allow it, this light and energy can even free us from the belief in consumerism, which feeds the greed that is destroying our planet.

In the simplicity of our human values—love and joy and hope, care for each other, care for the Earth—we are all connected together. But we can only discover this connection when we return to this simple core of being. Otherwise we will fall apart along with a world that has lost its center, a world that believes in its own advertising slogans. When we return to this potential of the heart, we will see what is being born, how a linking together of individuals, groups, and communities is taking place, how patterns of relationship are growing—and how life energy is flowing through these patterns. Once again humanity is recreating itself, creating a new civilization in the midst of the old.

In our focus on complexity we have overlooked the rule that the more complex something becomes, the more its energy becomes scattered and fragmented. Human beings have a unique role as the microcosm of the whole, which means that we can carry the whole multiplicity of creation within the simplicity of our essential nature. In this simplicity we carry life's oneness, and when we relate with love we relate to all of life.

When a human being is not scattered in the "ten thousand things," she is very powerful. This is a part of the purpose of spiritual practice: as we return to our essence we become more focused and able to claim our own power.

In the simple core of our being we carry the imprint of the Divine in all its miraculous nature. Because "God is a simple essence," life's divinity is able to express itself more directly in our love and joy and hope and other simple qualities. Reconnecting with these qualities, we reconnect with the divine within us and with the power of the Divine. When we live these qualities, we bring the power of the Divine into life. This power or energy can move through the patterns of relationship that are currently being created and can flow into life. In this simple way, life can regenerate itself.

The signs of this regeneration are all around us, in the way people are coming together. The internet and social media are an essential part of this process because they can connect people regardless of the barriers of physical location, race, background, nationality, or life experience. Different people in all parts of the world are linking together, forming networks of shared interests. Despite the dark drive to collect, manipulate, misuse our individual data, spread fake news, many of these communities are outside the control of any hierarchy or government. They belong to life itself.

New and diverse patterns of relationship are forming. We have yet to fully recognize that these patterns of relationship are so essential, that they are a real response to the problems and complexity of the times. They are not just for conveying information. They are creating a new, fast-changing, organic interrelationship of individuals and groups. Something is coming alive in a new way.

People are making connections on many different levels. We are linking together through global trade, travel, communication, conferences, and other forms of gatherings. In the last century the migration of spiritual paths and traditions from the East to the West worked at a deeper level to make a global connection, a merging of East and West, creating a light that is "neither of the East nor of the West."

We have yet to realize that this is all a part of the organism of life recreating itself on the pattern of oneness. We see these changes with the eyes of individuality and fragmentation that focus on the individual parts, still caught in the complex images of a decaying culture. The real picture is an emerging wholeness that is a life force in itself. *Life is reconnecting itself in order to survive and evolve.*

In these organic, non-hierarchical patterns of reconnection a new life force is flowing. This life force has the urgency that is needed if it is to survive and change at this time of crisis. It also has the power of oneness, and the simplicity of bringing people together. It is about sharing rather than possessiveness and isolation. It is the deep joy of knowing that we are one life. And it carries the imprint of divine oneness, which is stronger than any pattern of resistance.

PREPARING FOR THE STORM

How does the simplicity of life's new forms relate to the powerful shifts that are happening under the surface, the seismic dimension of outer changes? There is a beautiful balance in the way the organic patterns of life are complementing the changes in the depths, how human life on the surface is generating new forms to balance the inner shift.

These emerging patterns of interrelationship also serve a practical purpose. They are creating a container for new energy that is coming into life. This new life force is already surfacing through small fissures and cracks in the veneer of our civilization. It is generating new ideas, creating alternative ways of living.

But when new energy does not flow into new forms, it can constellate into conflict, in the old patterns of duality expressed in the outbreaks of terrorism and the power dynamics of repression. We are witnessing increased divisiveness, tribalism, different groups shouting that they are right. Social media that brings us together is also a megaphone for animosity and discord. Tragically, social media, and especially Facebook, was "weaponized" to fuel the systematic disinformation and persecution of the Rohingya in Myanmar, contributing to ethnic cleansing. What we are facing now is the emergence of a new archetypal energy, an energy that can create wonders, or take us into deeper suffering.

The archetypal world is a dimension of undifferentiated primal power. It can create great civilizations and terrible wars. An archetype that suddenly erupts into life can be devastating. Historically there have been examples of such moments, as when the wild force of Genghis Khan and his warriors destroyed the civilizations of the East. Genghis Khan constellated a powerful archetypal energy that initially manifested through violence and destruction.[3] But there are always signs that point to such dynamic shifts, signs that help humanity to go with the flow rather than resist the changes. Many families, like that of Rûmî the Sufi poet, migrated west before the Mongol hoards attacked.

The danger arises when we do not notice the signs. If we are too identified with the old ways and our position or identity within them, we will miss the chance to pack up a few possessions and move on. Resisting an emerging archetype will only lead to disaster. It may appear for a few years or decades that one can hold back the tide, clinging to one's old values and images of security, but a life based on denial of the real forces at work is often haunted by a sense of unreality, as must have been experienced in the last dying days of the Roman Empire. There is also an instinctual unease, a primal insecurity, which no amount of protection can dispel.

Much of our present insecurity comes from a deep knowing that our governments and cultures are planning for a future that will never happen. They may talk about economic expansion and increased prosperity, but we sense that these are just sand castles as the tide comes in. Human beings have an instinctual wisdom deeper than our conscious minds. We know that we are being lied to, but collectively we continue with our buying and selling, knowing no other way of life—even when our dreams are pointing to a different reality:

> A great storm is coming, the sky is darkening, a great wind tears the firmament apart with lightning and thunder. I wonder what is approaching. Am I watching people on a ship about to be tossed in a great sea and at the mercy of this storm?

Many people today have dreams of storms, tidal waves, and great devastation, and yet when we look around us at the shopping malls and well-stocked supermarkets, we see no cause for this fear. What do we do with our fear? What do we do with the part of us that is awakening to the possibilities and dangers that are coming?

The only response is to continue our daily life, because there is nowhere else to go, nothing else to do. In our global era there is no "safe place." This coming change will happen to the whole planet.

And yet we can be prepared; we can work to welcome the change. There is no point in stockpiling provisions or becoming self-sufficient. These are protectionist responses emanating from and perpetuating old patterns. Instead we can create a space within us so that the deep, instinctual knowing that belongs to our essential nature and to the Earth to which we are connected, can come to the surface. We can listen to our dreams and welcome a future that we do not yet know.

Mystics are prepared for this. We are used to standing on the edge of what is known and welcoming the unknown, the unknowable. We are trained to respond from a place within us deeper than any cultural conditioning—a place that belongs to the Divine. We try not to be imprisoned by any form or belief, and always allow our attachments to be swept aside by the greater power that comes from within. And we know that behind any apparent misfortune lie the love and care of our Beloved.

This attitude allows us to stand in the very axis of change, on the edge of the fault line, where we can help the new energy come into being. We are not frightened of devastation because we have already been destroyed by love. We are used to power greater than we can comprehend. And rather than being caught in outer dramas, in patterns of action and reaction, we have learned to rest in presence and stillness.

In the simplicity of our ordinary selves, living our ordinary lives, with our prayers and devotions we create a container that can help humanity make this transition. Rooted in the depth of our being we link together the inner and outer worlds so that the energy can flow more freely into the outer. And we do this not out of fear, which would contract us, but with love and joy to be of service, knowing that another cycle of revelation, another chapter in the story of our world, is unfolding.

FORCES OF TRANSFORMATION

That we live in unsure times is not just a cliché. Forces that have not been in our world for millennia are now present. Some of these forces, specifically oriented towards change and transformation, are here to help in this transition; there are energies, sparks of consciousness that have created the ideas behind some of the new technologies that have revolutionized our world, like the world wide web, the smartphone, solar panels. There are also new technologies, new ways of healing, waiting to be created, ideas that belong to the next era. The balance is always to bring them into the world without their true intention being devoured by the darkness of greed and worldly power.

Other forces are creating the foundations of the new age, working deep in the unconscious, constellating archetypal and spiritual patterns that will form the basis for the values and beliefs of the future, creating the sacred and healing symbols of the coming age. Still other forces are designed to disturb and destroy the present structures, those that belong to our hierarchical, patriarchal culture. Although these forces are necessary to clear away the past, they are less apparently beneficial and bring an energy of chaos and destruction. And then there are the forces of reaction and resistance, which are only too evident at this time, energies that draw our attention away from love, compassion, kindness, our basic human empathy.

Mostly we are unconscious of these forces; we feel their effects without knowing their true origin. We sense that something is changing, but often we react out of our fear or insecurity. Or we may become over-enthusiastic and in our excitement lose our center. Our groundlessness leaves us ineffective, and only makes matters worse.

We need both common sense and also a certain cunning to guide us. The ancient Greeks had a word for this quality of cunning: *metis*.[4] *Metis* was essential for sailors who needed to find their way through uncharted waters, and also for those who journeyed inward into the underworld. The forefathers of our Western culture regarded *metis* as a vital means for finding one's way in the unknown and the dark, for discovering the truth in a world of deception. We see cunning as a negative quality, as a means by which we cheat and are cheated. But surrounded, almost drowning in all the illusions of today, a quality of cunning can be a helpful quality.

Many illusions will come to the surface and be blown away. One of the primal illusions to resist is that of saving the world. The lover is here in service to her Beloved. We do not know what species need to survive, just as we do not know what new species will be born. We do not know what part of our civilization needs to be destroyed and what should be redeemed. We do not know what is a relic from the past, what belongs only to this time of transition, and what is part of the future. We do not know the purpose of this stage in our shared evolution. It is arrogance to think that we do.

We need to acknowledge that something is happening beyond our control. One of the features of our patriarchal culture is a desire to control our environment, and as a result we are fearful of what we cannot control. We are terrified of chaos, although anyone who has experienced real transformation knows that chaos is a necessary ingredient of true creativity. Without an element of chaos life stagnates.

Amidst these powerful forces that are reconstellating our life there are other, more minor energies awaking. They have a magical quality, and while some are beneficial, others are mischievous, not abiding by the rules of the status quo. They are a foretaste of the coming era when life's magical nature will resurface, as many of the barriers that separate the inner and outer worlds will fall away or be dissolved. We have forgotten or dismissed the magical nature of creation, but gradually the blinkers that have shielded us from this dimension of life will be removed.[5] We will find that our rational perception is quite inadequate to explain everything that is happening, and we will discover that we are part of a world full of the unexpected and unbelievable. Our present world seems so substantial and defined, but particle physics has shown it to be patterns of interrelating energies, as shamans have long understood.

Forces belonging to another dimension are also affecting us. These are forces that relate to our place within the cosmos. The evolutionary shift that is taking place concerns not just our planet in isolation. We are a part of an immense pattern of interrelated energies we call our galaxy. As we step into an awareness of oneness and the interrelationship of all of life here in this world, our perspective will begin to include the cosmos as a whole.

How these cosmic forces affect us is unknown, as it has been many millennia since we have experienced the direct impact of such transformative, evolutionary energies. But patterns of relationship are being created that stretch far beyond our individual planet.

We see only too easily the surface conflicts of our present time, and much work is needed to heal the wounds of our divided and abusive culture. But sadly our collective consciousness is very limited, aware of only a very small spectrum of the vastness in which we really live. There is a need to hold an awareness of what is beneath the surface, to sense, even if not to fully understand, the deeper forces at play. It is these forces and our response to them that determine our collective destiny. As I have mentioned, the changes we are beginning to experience have been building up for centuries, both the outer ecological crisis and the inner shift. We need to become pioneers of consciousness who can stand between the worlds, welcoming the energies of change. We may not get to fully experience these changes in our own short life, but we are working for seven or more generations.

For all those who care for the Earth and for their children, grandchildren, and souls yet to be conceived, this is work that is worthwhile, a real contribution. Many storms may come, both hurricanes that shake our physical world, and inner violence that can tear at the fabric of our civilization. Those who belong to love are prepared to travel light, to navigate these currents of the known and the unknown. Like the sailors who had only the stars and *metis* to guide them, we learn to read the signs in the world around us and in our dreams. In our practice and our presence we become part of these changes. We also bring a quality of love and consciousness to these inner energies, and in a subtle way help them to constellate into patterns that belong to the unfolding oneness.

This all may seem like a dream, a mirage in the desert of today's wasteland. But sometimes all we have is a dream to follow, a sign on the horizon, a hint within the heart.

THE RELATIONSHIP
BETWEEN THE WORLDS

The light of the body is the eye:
if therefore thine eye be single,
thy whole body shall be full of light.

Matthew 6:22

THE WORLD OF LIGHT AND THE
WORLD OF CREATION

We live in a multidimensional reality inhabited by beings in many different worlds invisible to our physical
senses. From the nature spirits—*devas* and elemental
beings formed from the energy and consciousness of the
Earth—to the spirit guides and angels made of pure light,
we are surrounded by these different fellow inhabitants.
Some cultures acknowledge their existence: the people in
South Asian countries traditionally built spirit houses to
welcome the protective spirit of the place; while in Japan
the Shinto religion worships the spirit world of the *kami*
who are manifestations of *musubi*, the interconnecting
energy of the universe. Many shamanic traditions work
directly with the elemental world, often for healing.
However, over the last centuries our Western world,
dominated by science and reason, has closed these doors

of perception and banished the spirit world to fairy tales and superstition—though Christianity has allowed our continued belief in angels. These worlds have been effectively censored from our inner sight and understanding. Collectively we no longer know how to communicate with their inhabitants.

Western science has explored the physical world to the smallest particle, but even though it may acknowledge atoms as interacting energy fields, it denies the existence of the inner worlds, creating a strange "flat earth" consciousness. Yet despite the density of our rational thought and its patterns of disbelief, the inner worlds still surround us, and there are indications that the walls between the worlds are becoming more permeable. As I have explored in *Spiritual Power*,[1] part of the spiritual work of the future will be communicating and working together with these inner realms, as the physician and shaman, the mystic and the scientist, come together and develop their knowledge and understanding.

As well as the inner worlds with elemental or angelic inhabitants, there are also the interior worlds of our own consciousness. There is our personal psyche that often surfaces in dreams or phobias, as well as the symbolic or archetypal world which belongs to our collective psyche, and can be explored through the faculty of active or creative imagination.[2] And there are the realms of light and love that belong to the soul or Self (*atman*). In Sufism the doors to these inner realms are found within the heart and open through spiritual practice. There are different degrees of divine light, greater depths of inner experience, as suggested by what Sufis call the different chambers of the heart.[3]

In the West in recent years there has been an increased interest in the knowledge and practice of shamanism, particularly how it can help in healing and reconnecting us with nature. There is less understanding of the worlds of light and how they work in relationship to our denser human nature. And while spiritual practice can give us direct access to our transcendent nature and higher centers of consciousness, the focus of much Western spiritual practice, such as mindfulness, is on being fully present and aware of the sensory world around us and within our physical, emotional bodies. We may believe in the intercession of angels, but the exact science of the light and consciousness of our own higher nature is rarely understood.

Human beings are unique in creation in that we have the potential to have access to all the different levels of reality. There is a spiritual teaching that when the soul comes into incarnation it passes through the different worlds, experiencing the different planes of existence before being born into the physical world. Later, through spiritual practice we are able to reconnect with these inner realms. Shamanic journeying may take us into the elemental or spirit world; or techniques like lucid dreaming's astral projection can give us out-of-body experiences of the subtle or intermediate realms. Meditation is the practice that gives us the most direct access to the realms of love and light which belong to our divine nature—the plane of the soul. If we are to use the spiritual potential within us not just for our own development but also in relation to the whole, it is helpful to understand how different realities relate together.

In my own Sufi tradition the work is primarily with the heart center that connects us to the divine light of the soul, and so it is our relationship with this reality that I will explore. Sufism has traditionally described the difference between the physical, instinctual world and the realms of light. The world of light is called the world of God's command (*'âlâm-e amr*), and the world we experience through the senses and the veils of the ego, the world of creation (*'âlâm-e kalq*).[4]

The world of God's command is quite different from the world of creation. The world of creation, which belongs to the four elements and is experienced mainly through our physical senses, appears governed by the laws of cause and effect, action and reaction. Our energy centers in the world of creation belong to our survival instinct with its forces of aggression and fear (fight or flight); to our sexual drive, which pulls us into the drama of desires; and to the drive for domination, which belongs to the will of the ego.[5] The drive for domination is also associated with providing for personal needs: food, clothing, and shelter. This world seems governed by will, while love—the most powerful force in creation—sadly appears more hidden. However recent understanding shows how cooperation rather than competition is often the most successful motivating force. Conflict is often present, but empathy is more powerful than we have been led to believe.

In the world of God's command love is the dominant force. In this inner world there is real harmony, and the peace that belongs to the soul. In its light there are no shadows in which deceptions can be born, no dance of appearances: we are seen as we really are and everything is known according to its true nature—"For now we see through a glass, darkly; but then face to face: now I know in part; but then shall I know even as also I am known."[6]

The world of God's command is a radiant, ever-expanding dimension of light upon light, a deepening immersion in divine oneness that leads to the complete absorption of individual consciousness in the most hidden Reality that is found in the innermost chamber of the heart (*akhfâ*). This is a Reality that permeates all of creation, all of existence and non-existence, and yet is veiled from any perception of consciousness. It is the simplest essence of life and also the greatest secret. Traditionally, the wayfarer aspires to awaken to the world of God's command and to be free from bondage to the world of creation—from the ego and its desires in the world of the senses, the dramas of success or failure, and other patterns of duality. The awakening of the spiritual centers within the individual, and the work of purification that precedes this awakening, are part of the process of liberation that belong to the spiritual journey. This journey involves the transformation of a human being from being attached to the world of the senses and identified with the ego, to the realization of union with God and our true nature as divine light and love.

Yet many wayfarers who have made the journey tell us that separation is the real illusion. The worlds may have difference qualities, but in reality they are united, permeated by the same essence. Nothing is higher or lower. All is One. The simplicity of this realization is so immense because everything is included. The darkness is divine darkness and the light divine light. This is not theory but a mystical realization. This oneness includes all the worlds of creation, as well as the mystical reality of the uncreated. The elemental beings, the *devas*, the angels, and human beings, as well as the butterflies, the bees, whales, and foxes, are all part of a living oneness—the matrix of creation.

Grounded in this realization, the mystic experiences creation *as it really is*. And with this awareness, the relationship between the worlds takes on a very different perspective.

Once we realize that everything is an aspect of the Divine, we experience how the world of creation fulfills its divine purpose, just as the world of light fulfills its purpose. Through the combination of the two worlds love's hidden nature can become known, unity be perceived in multiplicity. Rather than a sense of separation between the world of the senses and the world of light, we experience their interdependence. The physical world, the Earth, is central to the soul's unfolding experience of the Divine. Through the single eye of the heart we can perceive and participate in life's revelation of love.[7]

Awakening to the light of our higher nature helps us to fully experience the world of creation. Initially on the path the light within the heart is the guide that liberates us, helping us to see our faults and the hindrances that block us, then pointing out the path we need to follow. The light of the heart helps to show us our real destiny, which is often quite different from what we imagine. It helps to awaken us more fully to our true potential and the way we can be of service. Then, through this inner light, we are able to see this world as it really is, no longer blinded or blinkered by the desires of the ego. With the simplicity of our true self we are able to taste the strawberry, see the sunset, touch our lover.

The mystic brings together the worlds of the unseen and the seen, "viewing all things as proofs of divine unity" and "seeing God's outwardness in all things."[8] The inner worlds are no longer a place to escape from the confines of this world, but a quality of light, or awareness, that is needed to see the world as it truly is—to walk in a sacred manner, full of praise and thanksgiving. The way that the darkness of the world hides the divine light—its play of shadows, desires, and ignorance—is a revelation as unique as the way the inner worlds appear to reveal the light. Both worlds are in service to the wonder of God's creation. And we are a witness to the beauty and power of this living oneness.

INTERPENETRATING WORLDS

In the past era mystical consciousness developed a profound understanding of the inner worlds, experiencing dimensions of light and absorption in God (or for Buddhist mystics, *nirvana*). These inner realities were often experienced as quite separate from experiences of the outer world, and many mystics lived in monasteries or hermitages, isolated from the demands of life. Even in Sufism, which is not a monastic path, the emphasis was on turning away from the outer world to discover the inner truth within the heart. This inner orientation belonged to an era that stressed a transcendent divinity, often at the expense of the immanent qualities of the Divine—particularly those that belong to the feminine and the physical world.

As we enter a new era, we are noticing a shift towards including everyday life and the physical world in spiritual practice. In the West many people who are attracted to spiritual life are unable or unwilling to embrace the life of a renunciate. Monasticism has lost its appeal. Is this a cultural trend, a lack of serious spiritual commitment in our Western world? Is the grip of materialism so strong that we cannot leave behind our worldly attachments?

Or could this shift be part of a new pattern of spiritual awareness that does not seek to separate the inner and outer, the spiritual and worldly? Perhaps we are moving towards an awareness of oneness that embraces all of life, the light and the dark, the world of God's command and the world of creation.

As a new chapter in the sacred story of life is being written the patterns of revelation change. And so does the work of the wayfarer, the way we work to reveal divine light within ourself and the world. The trends we are experiencing as a spiritual collective are signs of a new revelation. We will come to see how the worlds of divine light interpenetrate the world of creation, how they are not separate dimensions, but different facets of a oneness that continually reveals and hides itself.

Those who have made the journey into the heart of hearts know the love that is at the core of life, the love that gives meaning and magic to every breath. One of the paradoxes of life is that the inner reality of light and love is present all around us, in every breath we breathe, and yet it is hidden, veiled by the ego. It is the real substance of life, the inner secret of creation. It is our natural self which we have forgotten, the paradise from which we have been banished, where we walked naked in the presence of God.

Why should this simple truth remain hidden? Does humanity have to remain exiled from its own essential nature? Or can we reclaim this paradise, this simple and joyful sense of what is real, as part of the natural fabric of everyday life? Then we might begin to see that the worlds do not have to appear separate, and the reality of light can be present even in the shadows of the world of creation.

The traditional response is that this dimension of light and love is only accessible to those who have renounced the ego and purified their lower nature. If our lower nature imprisons us in the world of creation, then we have to leave it behind. But does this mean that the doors of revelation are only open to a few, and the world as a whole must remain shrouded in darkness, a wasteland dying from humanity's greed and forgetfulness?

Life needs the pure light of the inner world; it needs this love and power to purify and protect it. The wayfarer knows that only in the light of what is real can we find our way, can we reclaim the source of life: "For with Thee is the fountain of life: in Thy light shall we see light."[9]

The work of the mystic is to bring this light into life. With our help, the light of divine love can awaken in the midst of our present collective patterns; it can begin to redeem our world and help restore the joy, beauty, and wonder that have been lost.

BEYOND A PARADIGM OF OPPOSITES

Does the paradigm of opposites really hold up if we look at it closely? There are the primal opposites of night and day, life and death: but how often is the nighttime completely dark, the day without shadows? Life and death are part of each other, part of the continual flow of creation, and each moment we die and each moment we are born. Transformation is both a death and a birth, and in the real wholeness of a human being we realize how the many parts of ourself come together.

The newly awakening oneness does not reveal itself through contrasting pairs of opposites but through patterns of relationship, relationships built upon similarities rather than opposition. Once we clear away the paradigm of opposition, we will encounter a very different picture of a life that is multihued, with each color expressing a different aspect of divine beauty. If our eyes are open, we can see this global shift around us in our city streets with all the different peoples, the mixture of races, with all the different music that is being played, the different customs and religions: so many ways to worship the One. Something has changed that is fundamental, and yet we overlook it, or choose to ignore what it means. Despite our political systems, fundamentalist religions, or racial ideologies, the world is no longer a place we can divide into opposites.

The old ways remain present; the dynamics of duality will take decades to die. But the secret is to look to what is being born. The emerging patterns of relationship carry the new energy of life, the energy that is coming into being and will transform our planet.

My own path has taken me deep within the heart, but it has not been about escaping the physical world, but rather being at the place where the worlds meet, where light comes into life and the heart learns to sing. It is this coming together of the worlds that has been the central note of my journey. Rather than trying to be fully immersed in the light, I have been drawn to understand how the worlds resonate, how pure light is reflected in this outer world, and how in this dance of reflection new patterns of creation can emerge. Grief and joy are still present, and awareness of the light brings its own sorrow—the deepest sadness for me is how people cover their own light, preferring the shadows of the ego to the beauty of their real nature—as Rûmî says "How can you sell yourself for so little, you who are so precious in God's eyes?"

Human nature has many qualities, both kindness and cruelty. The world of light is pure love. But when the worlds come together something else is also present, born from this meeting. And I sense that this new quality belongs to the next era of evolution. Whether we are working together with the nature *devas* or the light of the soul, a relationship is being formed, and it is these relationships that carry the new note. And if this meeting of the worlds is for the sake of the whole, of the Earth Herself, then this new note belongs to the song of creation coming alive in a new way.

Life is recreating itself through us. The life force working through us is uncovering patterns of relationship that belong to wholeness, that belong to life systems founded upon interrelationship and interdependence. We know how these patterns form the ecological basis of life. In past centuries we have focused on the Darwinian model of struggle for survival, and all of the dynamics of competition that relate to this perspective. And life does have forces of aggression, domination, and competition. But in recent years our understanding has shifted to recognize that the biosphere can be seen as a "cooperative communal venture among all living organisms."[10] For example, forests—which were once seen as composed of individual trees competing for water, nutrients, and sunlight—have now been understood as a single living organism connected by underground fungal networks forming cooperative, interdependent relationships, maintained by communication and a collective intelligence similar to an insect colony.[11]

Ecology is teaching us how no living organism exists in isolation and nature sustains life by creating patterns of relationship. This shift in our understanding belongs not just to the biosphere, but all the interrelated patterns of our multidimensional world. Each organism is part of a deeper wholeness in which all forms of life coexist together. Now we need to consciously reclaim these deeper patterns, recognize the ways life-forms, different peoples, and different worlds can interrelate and nourish each other. One example is the way in the last decades the East has enriched the West with its spiritual knowledge and practices, bringing what I have described as a new color into our spectrum of consciousness.

This may seem a simplistic approach to the many problems of the present, and we have witnessed how the energy of globalism can seem to get hijacked by the forces of competition and greed, how it has also brought terrorism to our doorstep, as well as fear of migrants. We cannot avoid these shadow-dynamics; the danger comes when our reactions just reinforce protectionism and the images of duality, "us" and "them." Sadly, it is these darker images that attract the attention of our media and create collective anxiety.

But this is really a distraction from the real need of the moment: life is recreating itself on a global level and it needs our participation. Those of us who can journey inward, who can see beyond the horizons of a purely physical world, are needed where the worlds come together. As I have mentioned there are many different worlds, and I have focused on the relationship between the worlds of light and the physical world, because this belongs to the Sufi tradition I have practiced for half a century. But I firmly believe that we need to relate and communicate with the inhabitants of other worlds. A relationship with the nature *devas*, who carry the consciousness and original wisdom within nature, is needed to help heal and transform our ravaged world—we can no longer afford to live in isolation from their power and primal understanding of the Earth and the laws of nature.[12] And anyone who has felt the beauty and power of the angelic world knows how valuable their presence can be. Is it too simple a statement to say that at this time of global crisis we need all the help we can get?

Sadly shamans do not play a central role in our ecological debate, despite the warning the Kogi Mamas gave to their "young brothers" about ecological catastrophe and the imbalance of the Earth's ecosystem. Communicating with nature *devas* is not part of our contemporary curriculum, and we have little understanding of the angelic world or how to relate to these beings of light. But we can learn to be receptive to the inner worlds, to acknowledge their existence and welcome the unseen. My sense is that in coming centuries the doors between the worlds will open further, and we will relearn our original wisdom. Or, as in the Biblical story of Jacob's ladder, we will come to the place where the angels ascend and descend to Earth.

If we are present in the moment, we will naturally find ourself aligned with the emerging patterns of life: life will speak to us in our own way because we are a part of life. Despite our patterns of resistance, life will align us with what is needed. If we try to create our future or hold onto the past, we will remain stuck in the images of what is dying. But as most spiritual disciplines teach us, only by being present can we be awake to what is real: only in the present moment can we participate in what is really happening and not just perpetuate the images of our fears and desires.

In the present moment we can discover how the inner and outer are being realigned and are waiting for us to live the connection. The mystic, the lover, lives the link of love between the worlds. We are this connection, the place where the light comes from the inner to the outer, where the angels can once again speak to us. We are the higher and the lower, and we are the oneness that embraces both. When two realities come together, they start to spin, to move together in a way quite different from the dynamics of dualism. Through their union something new can be born, a way of being that is the future. This is what is waiting to happen. The union of the two is like an alchemical marriage through which the individual will begin to realize her real potential as microcosm of the whole, as well as a part of an interrelated web of life and light. We are the one and the many. This is the next level of realization of individual consciousness.

THE LIGHT OF THE WORLD

The world of God's command is not separate from the world of creation. Without its higher spiritual centers, the world of creation would be a pale shadow of itself, a place absent of divine love. Without the dense planes of manifestation, there would be nothing to reflect the pure light, and our Beloved would remain hidden as an inward essence. In the wonder of life's multiplicity, in love's many forms, the self-revelation of the Divine takes place. It is the light of the higher worlds reflected in the lower worlds that makes this possible. The purpose of our incarnation is to help in this work, to combine the worlds in our prayers and loving, to plant these seeds of light into the earth.

When a soul is born, it brings with it its pure light. This is one of the reasons that there is such joy in the birth of a child: we recognize in it life's divine nature. Through the presence of the child for an instant we remember life as it really is. In the memory of humanity lives a time when we all lived in this paradise, in the simple joy of being alive, when the light of our spiritual self was not hidden. It is sometimes called the "Golden Age." But just as the developing ego of the child veils it from the light of what is real, so did the gift of individual consciousness force us from paradise. We still carry the scars of that apparent abandonment.

Since the Golden Age, eras have come and gone. The most recent era has witnessed the development over centuries of a powerful focus on a masculine, transcendent divinity, which has emphasized the separation between the worlds. This has had a very real effect on different levels. Spiritually it has formed the image of a spiritual journey away from the world, but also it has created a denser veil between the physical and the inner worlds, a barrier that exists both within individual consciousness and in the world itself. This veil has become almost impenetrable over the past centuries, partly due to our rational culture and our pursuit of materialism.

The density of the veil has made it more difficult for the light, the magic and meaning of the inner worlds to be seen in the outer world, and for the love of the inner to nourish the outer. We know how hard we have to struggle to reclaim the light of our true nature. We are less aware of how the Earth itself has been separated from its source in the inner: it too has been starved of a certain essential nourishment—as a result the light of the sacred is fading.

Just as we need the light of our higher nature to find our way, so does the Earth need this light to awaken to its true purpose. Our imprisonment of the Earth in dense clouds of materialism and forgetfulness has deprived it of its magical nature. The magical nature of creation is essential to its survival and transformation.

The light from the world of pure love can awaken the magical nature of life, just as it awakens an individual to the miraculous Earth in which we really live. In the light of divine love we can see and participate in a world which is a dynamic, spiritual being full of the wondrous and unexpected. Without this light we see only the world of our senses, a world we have raped and made destitute and left clinging to the edge of its survival. We see a world defined by our ego and its desires, rather than a place of unlimited possibilities whose very nature is sacred.

We remain attached to our limited perception of life because we have imagined a world that we can control. The past era has taken us down this road of domination. Christianity taught that we were given dominion over nature. Then the Catholic Church focused on worldly power rather than spiritual awareness, consolidating its power through persecuting the Gnostics, Cathars and other mystics, burning women who had healing powers, and suppressing many of the esoteric teachings of Christ. Those who did not adhere to its hierarchy were tortured as heretical.

We remain frightened of the unknown, yet the Divine is the greatest unknown. In banishing God to heaven, we have created the illusion of being in power on Earth. The developments of science have worked to enhance the illusion, describing a world we could master with reason and technology. If we welcome the Divine back into the Earth, into the midst of everyday life, we will no longer be able to dominate by force and will, to sustain the illusion of control. We will have to relearn how to be in relationship with the Divine in everyday life, just as we will have to relearn our relationship with the Earth—restore reverence and real care, recognize that we are just a part of a living community. This loss of a sense of control is at the root of our resistance to any real collective awakening.

But despite the density of our denial, as I have mentioned, the veils between the worlds are beginning to lift. The magic of life can be found in unexpected places. Individuals can have sudden spiritual awakenings, that initial moment of grace as the light comes through. And darker forces have also found their way into our collective—not all elemental beings are benevolent. Because we do not recognize their existence, we can easily just blame their effect on the greed of corporations or policies of governments or dictators. Nor do we understand how some energies encourage cruelty, feed off human suffering. If we are to evolve into spiritual maturity we will need to learn to recognize the existence and origins of different forces, discriminate between the worlds. But first we need to step out of the insularity of our present "flat world" consciousness. As Hamlet said to his rational friend, "There are more things in heaven and earth, Horatio, than are dreamt of in thy philosophy."[13]

PATTERNS OF RELATIONSHIP

Living a relationship between the worlds means stepping into a more ambiguous, less defined world, as well as reclaiming the wisdom of the feminine, who instinctively understands life's interconnected wholeness—the patterns of relationship that nourish us in both the seen and unseen worlds. Sadly it may take generations for us to fully reconnect with the knowing of our ancestors, who lived more easily in a fluid reality of inner and outer worlds. We have little understanding of how our western consciousness has been censored over the centuries, how we have been systematically denied part of our heritage. The Christian banishment of the pagan world, its chopping down the sacred groves, does not just belong to our history books, but continues to effect us.

Also it will be a revolution as profound as Galileo's observation that the Sun does not go around the Earth. We have created a myth that human beings are the sole carriers of consciousness, the masters of the world around us. Awakening to a multidimensional reality inhabited by beings with different powers and qualities of consciousness, different ways of communicating and patterns of behavior, could be both wonderful and deeply threatening.

When I was nineteen and stepped into my teacher's room I found myself in a space full of the unseen—the air was thick with the presence of other levels of reality. It was place of miracles, both of healing and opening of hearts. Prayers were alive and angels existed. Since then I have been able to see a little of the worlds that surround us, experience the guidance and grace that comes from within. I would no longer know what it means to live on a single plane of consciousness, isolated, alone. Collectively we have so many channels on our television, so many apps on our smart phones, but we live in a shrinking consciousness focused on materialism. And all around us are other realities waiting to communicate.

A few years ago I was walking along the beach, sunlight sparkling on the ocean waves, when suddenly I was taken out of my physical body into the world of light. I found myself surrounded by beings of light and they were very puzzled. They told me that it was supposed to be a time when the different worlds and their inhabitants came together, communicated with each other. They did not understand why we had retreated into an insularity of consciousness rather than being open to this relationship. They left me with the saying, "It was not supposed to be like this." The angelic world has a very different relationship to time than exists in our world—our sense of time often does not have any meaning for them. But they knew that this was a moment in time when the worlds were supposed to come together, and that there were certain opportunities in this opening. As I walked back along the beach I was left with their sense of puzzlement, and the possibility of a missed opportunity.

And yet there are those among us who are open to this opportunity, who have felt the presence of the inner worlds, experienced the light of the plane of the soul. Many have been drawn into a shamanic experience, discovering their power animal or spirit guide.[14] Just to awake to an awareness of relating to other planes of existence is an important step, breaking free from the confines of our collective consciousness. In my understanding it is these patterns of relationship that are pivotal. Specific guidance and help is always beneficial, healing is a gift. But through these patterns, interconnections, a new quality of consciousness can be born. Just as our awareness of the interconnections of the ecosystem shifts us towards an understanding of the ways of oneness—how the biosphere communicates and cooperates—so an openness to the inner worlds will expand our consciousness in unforeseen ways, no longer banishing ourselves from a garden of miracles and magic. And central to this shift in our evolution is a relationship to the Earth as a living, spiritual being whose inhabitants belong to both the seen and unseen realms.

ANIMA MUNDI

AWAKENING THE SOUL OF THE WORLD

*God redeems humanity, but nature needs
to be redeemed by human alchemists, who are
able to induce the process of transformation,
which alone is capable of liberating the
light imprisoned in physical creation.*

Stephan Hoeller[1]

The world is a living spiritual being. This was understood by the ancient philosophers and the alchemists who referred to the spiritual essence of the world as the *anima mundi*, the "Soul of the World." They regarded the World Soul as a pure ethereal spirit diffused throughout all nature, the divine essence that embraces and energizes all life in the universe.

A similar understanding of the spiritual nature of creation has long been held by Indigenous people, whose shamans often worked to care for the spiritual energy that sustains the flourishing of life. For example the Kogi Mamas (priests) of the Sierra Nevada learn to connect and interact with *Aluna*, a cosmic consciousness that is like the mind of nature, the source of all life and collective intelligence.

However, throughout history our understanding of the world as a living being with a spiritual essence has dramatically changed. Plato understood that "the cosmos is a single Living Creature which contains all living creatures within it."[2] While this tradition was carried on by the Gnostics and later the alchemists, the church fathers imaged a world that was neither divine nor sacred. A transcendent divinity was the source of all creation, and humanity lived in exile from heaven in a state of sin. This doctrine created a split between matter and spirit, causing the world to be seen as separate from its creator.

The understanding of the world as sacred resurfaced from time to time over the next centuries. In the Gothic movement of the twelfth century, and later in the Renaissance, the created world was briefly seen through the image of the World Soul. In their cathedrals the Gothic architects reflected their vision of a sacred order within creation that belongs to this feminine divine principle. The World Soul animated and formed nature according to divine proportions, which the architects, masons, sculptors, and stained-glass artists imaged in their creations.[3]

Again during the Renaissance nature was briefly seen as a living spiritual essence:

> If medieval theology had removed God to a wholly transcendent sphere, to the Renaissance Platonists nature was permeated by life, divinity, and numinous mystery, a vital expression of the World Soul and the living powers of creation. In the words of Richard Tarnas, "The garden of the world was again enchanted, with magical powers and transcendent meaning implicit in every part of nature."[4]

In the Renaissance the World Soul was understood as a spiritual essence within creation, guiding the unfolding of life and the cosmos. In the words of the Renaissance philosopher Giordano Bruno, the World Soul "illumines the universe and directs nature in producing her species in the right way."[5] The World Soul was also the creative principle that the Renaissance artists sought to channel in their work. Their art was based upon the same sacred proportions they saw in nature, and they understood the imagination as a magical power that can "lure and channel the energies of the *anima mundi*."

The Renaissance left us great wonders of art and the imagination. It was a brief flowering, however. The orthodoxies of the church reestablished the split between matter and spirit, and the rise of science began to image the natural world as a machine whose disembodied workings human beings could rationally understand and master. The magical world of creative mystery infused with divine spirit became a dream belonging only to poets and the laboratories and symbolic writings of the alchemists.

The alchemists continued to explore the *anima mundi*. While the church looked for light in the heavens, the alchemists sought the light hidden in matter. They understood that there was a sacred essence in the fabric of creation, which through their experiments and imagination they worked to release. For the alchemists the *anima mundi* is the divine spark in matter, the "philosophical Mercury," which is the "universal and scintillating fire in the light of nature, which carries the heavenly spirit with it."

Alchemy is concerned with turning lead into gold, liberating the light hidden in the darkness—"the fiery sparks of the world soul, i.e. the light of nature ... dispersed or sprinkled throughout the structure of the great world into all fruits of the elements everywhere."[6] The alchemists also understood that there is a connection between the *anima mundi* and the soul or innermost secret of man. The source of the wisdom and knowledge of the all-pervading essence of the *anima mundi* was "the innermost and most secret *numinosum* of man."[7]

In the last century Carl Jung rediscovered the wisdom of the alchemical *opus* and showed how alchemical symbols image the process of inner transformation that can release this hidden light. Jung differentiated between two forms of spiritual light: *lumen dei*, the light proceeding from the spiritual realm of a transcendent God; and *lumen naturae*, the light hidden in matter and the forces of nature. The Divine Light may be experienced through revelation and spiritual practices that give us access to our transcendent Self. The Light of Nature needs to be released through inner alchemy so that it can work creatively in the world.

The tradition of alchemy reinterpreted into the language of inner transformation is a key to help us to liberate our natural light and to transform the world. The alchemical light hidden in darkness is our own light, which is also the divine spark within matter. Our natural light is part of the light of the World Soul. This alchemical unlocking of matter can be associated with freeing, or awakening, the World Soul, the *anima mundi*. As a microcosm of the whole, the individual can participate directly in the alchemical process that liberates this light, a light that is needed to understand the mysteries of creation and the ways of working with its magical nature. With the *lumen naturae* we can once again learn how to unlock the secrets of nature, so that we no longer have to attack and destroy the natural world in order to survive.

Alchemy is our Western tradition of inner transformation. Sufis have always known about the inner process of alchemy.[8] One of the early Sufi masters, Dhû-l-Nûn, was described as an alchemist, and a great twelfth-century Sufi, al-Ghazzâlî, titled one of his most important books *The Alchemy of Happiness*. Sufis have mastered the alchemy of the heart, through which the energy of love transforms the individual to reveal the light hidden within the darkness of the *nafs* or lower self. They developed a detailed science (described in the following chapter, "The Light of the Heart") for working with the chambers of the heart to effect an inner transformation that gives the wayfarer access to the light of his true nature. This work does not belong just to the individual, but can have a direct relationship to the whole of creation and the heart of the world. Once we recognize the mysterious connection between our own innermost essence and the Soul of the World, we can use the tools of inner transformation to work directly with the Soul of the World, to help the *anima mundi* reveal its divine light and awaken.

AS ABOVE SO BELOW

As a result of Jung's writings on alchemy, we have begun to understand the nature of the inner alchemical work. The work on the alchemical lead—the *prima materia*, that which is "glorious and vile, precious and of small account and is found everywhere"[9]—is the work on the *shadow*, the rejected and unacknowledged parts of our psyche. The philosopher's stone, the gold made from the lead, is our own true nature, the Self. Rather than a transcendent, disembodied divinity, alchemy reveals a divine light that exists in the very depths of our psyche. This light hidden in darkness, the *lumen naturae*, is also our instinctual self and natural way of being, which until it is revealed is covered over by patterns of conditioning and the layers of the false self.

What is the difference between the light discovered in the depths of the psyche and the light of our transcendent divine Self glimpsed in meditation or other experiences? *It is the same light* experienced in different ways. The Sufis know that the Beloved, the source of all light, has both an immanent and a transcendent quality. He whom we love is both "nearer to him than his jugular vein" and "beyond even his idea of the beyond." The Self, "larger than large and smaller than small," has the same dual quality.

The yogi deep in meditation and the alchemist in his laboratory are seeking the same light, the same divine nature. Everything that we experience has a dual nature, a masculine and a feminine aspect, and the same is true of the light of the Self. It can be experienced in its masculine form as a pure transcendent light, consciousness without the constrictions of the psyche or the physical world. In meditation we can first glimpse and then rest in our eternal and infinite nature, and come to know a reality not defined or constricted by our body or the manifest world. This is a reality of light upon light, our colorless and formless essence.

We can also come to know our divine nature in its feminine, embodied nature, as the light of being, our natural wisdom, the gold of our true nature. In this light we experience and know the divine within creation, the way our Beloved reveals Herself in a multitude of forms, each form a different expression of one infinite being. We see how each color, each smell, every taste, even every thought and feeling, is a unique expression of the Divine. In this way we come to know our Beloved in creation in a way that is hidden in the transcendent. In this revelation we see that each thing is unique and that all things are one, and we discover the relationship of the parts to the whole—the interconnected wonder of creation. We see the rich tapestry of life and know that it is one Being revealing Itself in so many ways.

If we are not to remain in the paradigm of duality—living our inherited split between masculine and feminine, spirit and matter—we need to acknowledge both of these aspects. We cannot afford to follow the footsteps of the patriarchal church fathers and seek only a transcendent light, look only towards heaven. We also need to know the light hidden in matter and understand the magic of creation that it reveals. We need to know the mysteries of creation as celebrated in the most sacred text of the alchemists, the *Emerald Tablet*, attributed to Hermes Trismegistos:

> What is below is like that which is above, and what is above is like that which is below, to accomplish the miracles of the one thing.[10]

The light hidden in matter is the one light experienced within the mystery of creation, the hidden treasure revealed through the dance of multiplicity. The creation of the manifest world is a revelation of the hidden nature of the Divine, as expressed in the *hadîth*, "I was a hidden treasure and I longed to be known, so I created the world." But we can only experience the wonder and know the true nature of this revelation through the light hidden within it. Just as our Beloved has hidden love's secret within us—"Man is My secret and I am his secret"—so is the Divine hidden within creation. Sometimes, in moments amidst the beauty or glory of nature, in the vastness of the stars or the perfection of the early morning dew on a flower, we glimpse this wonder. The light hidden in matter breaks through and we stand in awe before our Creator, as reflected in the words of the poet Gerard Manley Hopkins:

The world is charged with the grandeur of God.
It will flame out, like shining from shook foil.[11]

Through this light we can awaken to the sacred nature
of life and experience the real beauty of divine revelation. There is only one light—"as above so below"—and
yet the *lumen naturae* has a different quality to the *lumen
dei*, allowing a different quality of revelation. The light
that is discovered in the depths of the psyche, through
the work on the shadow and the inner alchemical *opus*,
reveals part of our divine nature that is hidden from a
purely transcendent consciousness. We come to know
ourself and our Beloved in a new way. For each of us
this revelation is unique. Part of the wonder of creation
is how She offers a different experience to each of us;
even the same apple tasted by two people will be a different experience. Through the light within nature we
can see life as it really is, a moment by moment experience—each moment as unique as a snowflake. At the
same time we experience each unique moment as part
of a greater oneness—the mandala of life. We see the
patterns that connect together all of life; and how each
part reflects the whole.

Whoever can't see the whole in every part plays
    at blind man's bluff;
A wise man tastes the Tigris in every sip.[12]

CONNECTIONS OF LIGHT

In our deeper knowing we understand this deep con-
nectedness of all of life. And yet the church, the rise of
Western science, and a growing culture of materialism
have effectively banished the *anima mundi* from our

collective imagination, until we lost this primal relationship. In the words of Jung, "man himself has ceased to be the microcosm and his anima is no longer the consubstantial *scintilla* or spark of the *anima mundi*, the World Soul."[13] How can we now redeem this relationship, recreate this connection in our imagination and inner work? How can we return our light to the World Soul?

Once we make the simple acknowledgment that we are a part of the whole, then a connection is made between our light and the world. We make this connection with our consciousness and with our imagination; then through this connection our light begins to flow. In this way we begin to redeem the work of the whole. These connections create pathways of light that find their way through the darkness of the collective psyche. Just as in our personal psyche, there are blocks and places of resistance to this flow of light; and there are also places of power, creativity, and unexpected qualities.

The World Soul is not a fixed or defined substance, but a living substance made out of the hopes, dreams, and deepest imaginings of humanity and of all creation. This is the home of creation's collective memories and the myths of humanity. Here are the archetypes and powers that define our life. Here are hidden places of magical meaning, places where dreams can come into being. We have lived for so long in the stark barrenness of a rational landscape that we have forgotten the potency that lies beneath the surface. Flowing through the pathways created by our conscious connection to the *anima mundi*, our light will find its way to places of power that are within the world, places where deeper layers of meaning are waiting to come alive.

We presently see the material world as something apart from ourselves, a solid and enduring object without life or magic. Like the seventeenth-century scientists who decided animals had no feelings and thus could be dissected without suffering, we feel free to inflict our will upon our world, pillaging it for our own gain without any thought to the suffering and damage we are subjecting it to. Caught up in our materialistic drives, we may not recognize that this image of the world is an illusion, an insubstantial dream that can easily alter or dissolve as new forces come into play. As our light makes its connections within the World Soul, it will activate some of these forces, energies that are waiting to liberate the world from this destructive illusion. We know how this works in our own alchemical journey, how what we find beneath the surface changes our values in unexpected ways, how connections are then made and synchronicities occur that before would have been unbelievable. As we make these connections, we will begin to see that the world and our own selves both are more magical than we know.

This work of connecting our light to the world does not need to be done through a mass movement, or by millions of people. For centuries a few alchemists held these secrets of inner transformation against the powerful forces of the church and the establishment. The real work is always done by a small number of individuals. What matters is the level of participation: whether we dare to make a real commitment to the work of the soul. Unlike the alchemists living in their laboratories, we do not need to give up our ordinary outer life—everyday life can also be a necessary balance and protection against the strange delusions so easily created by the inner world. But we do need to recognize that there is a certain work that needs to be done, and that we can no longer stand on the sidelines and watch our collective dreams spin out of control.

Our culture may have isolated us within our individual self, separated us from the magic of life—but once again this is just a surface mirage. We are all connected and part of the living substance of creation. Within every cell of our being, every spark of consciousness, we have a knowing of oneness. Our own inner journey cannot be separate from the journey of the whole. An inner journey separate from the whole is no real journey; it is just another illusion created by an ego that wants to protect itself.

The substance of our soul is part of the fabric of life, the tapestry of creation in which are woven the unicorns and monsters of our dreams as well as the skyscrapers of our cities. The inner and outer worlds are not separate—despite all the efforts of our rational culture to have us believe they are. The recent dramas of terrorism have once again brought demons into our living rooms, and we sense there is nowhere really safe from these shadows. But we do not need to simply be victims of these archetypal nightmares. By evoking the real magic that comes from within, we can work to balance the light and the dark, and creatively participate in changing the dreams that define our collective life.

The light of the World Soul is waiting to be used to connect us with the inner powers that belong to matter and to life itself. The real world is an enchanted place, full of magical powers waiting to be used. And, as the alchemists understood, the *anima mundi* is a creative force: "it is the artist, the craftsperson, the 'inner Vulcan' which shapes and differentiates the prime matter, giving it form."[14]

AWAKENING TO THE PURPOSE OF CREATION

The World Soul is not just a psychological or philosophical concept. It is a living spiritual substance within us and around us, what the Kogis call the mind of nature. Just as the individual soul pervades the whole human being—our body, thoughts, and feelings—the nature of the World Soul is that it is present within everything. It pervades all of creation, and is a unifying principle within the world. The alchemist-physician Thomas Browne saw it as "the Universal Spirit of Nature, the *anima mundi* or World Soul responsible for all phenomena and which binds all life together."[15] Marsilio Ficino saw the World Soul flourishing everywhere:

> The soul is all things together.... And since it is the center of all things, it has the forces of all. Hence it passes into all things. And since it is the true connection of all things, it goes to the one without leaving the others.... therefore it may rightly be called the center of nature, the middle term of all things, the face of all, the bond and juncture of the universe."[16]

The Soul of the World permeates all of creation like salt in water. The physical world is the denser plane, and within it and sustaining it is the reality of the soul, which contains the Higher Intelligence that is the creative and ordering principle of life.

This divine intelligence is in everything. It is the spark within matter, the light within a human being. When we isolate ourself from our own soul, we deny ourself conscious access to this light, to its guidance and intelligence. Then our life becomes without meaning or purpose, "a walking shadow ... signifying nothing." Without real purpose, our life is just a physical existence. When we reconnect with our soul, the magic and meaning of life come alive both within us and around us.

Our real gift to life is an awareness of its sacred purpose. When we are aware of life's purpose, the light of the soul shines in our life, and its secret hidden within the world comes alive. And the light that is within us is within everything; it is "at the center of all things." When our light comes alive within us, it comes alive within all of creation. It reveals to creation its true purpose. At the present time our collective culture sees life primarily from a material perspective—we worship the god of consumerism, making acquisition our life's goal. We are imprisoned within matter. We have forgotten the symbolic and sacred meaning of the outer world. Alienated from our soul, we have alienated creation from its deeper meaning. And because we have denied the world its sacred nature, it is slowly dying.

The real alchemical work is to liberate creation from this imprisonment—to awaken life to its meaning. We have to free the light that is within us and within the world. A transcendent image of the Divine will only give us access to a transcendent light. We need the light hidden in matter, the gold that is within lead. When this light comes alive within life, it can change the patterns of creation and create the forms of the future that will bring life back into harmony. It can manifest its unifying nature.

The alchemists understood the nature of this light:

> It is the father of every miraculous work in the
>   whole world....
> Its power is perfect if it is converted to earth.[17]

Working within the world, this power *is* the light and power of the Divine made manifest. The light that is within our own psyche *is* the light within the *anima mundi*. In the depth of ourself we discover this essential oneness. This is the same awareness as the yogi's realization that one's true nature and unchanging self (*atman*) is the Universal Self (*Atman*). What is within us is within everything. Once we understand this truth, we step outside of the parameters of our individual self and come to realize the power that is within us. This shift in awareness is a very simple step that has profound consequences.

IMAGINING THE WORLD

At the moment, the world is asleep, suffering the dreams of humanity, which have become a nightmare of desecration and pollution. In our hubris we have forgotten that the world is more than our collective projections, that it is more mysterious and strange than our rational minds would like us to believe. Quantum physics has revealed a fluid and unpredictable world, in which consciousness and matter are not separate—whether a photon of light behaves as a particle or wave depends upon the consciousness of the observer. But we remain within the images of Newtonian physics: matter that is dead, definable, and solid; and consciousness that is objective, safely divorced from the physical world. Matter and spirit remain split, and we continue in the patriarchal fantasy that we can have control over our world.

As we have already seen, the physical world was not always experienced as so isolated. Many cultures have been more concerned with the relationship between the worlds. In the medieval imagination the physical world was just one part of the Great Chain of Being. Medieval cathedrals imaged a symbolic and geometric relationship between the different parts, with the maze that symbolized our journey through this world mirroring the rose window's image of a higher reality of light. In the Sufism of Ibn 'Arabî, the worlds were seen as connected by the symbolic world of the imagination, which acts as a bridge or an "intermediary between the world of Mystery (*'âlâm al-ghayb*) and the world of Visibility (*'âlâm al-shahâdat*)."

In their retorts and crucibles the alchemists were working not just with chemical substances but also with the inner energies of life. Their symbolic writings describe both the mixture of tinctures and the marriage of the king and queen, the union of Sun and Moon. The alchemists took their work seriously, knowing the real responsibility involved.[18] They knew that they were working with a secret substance in life, "mercury" or "quicksilver," a catalyst that can transform whatever it touches. The way their chemicals changed and transformed imaged how life can be changed with the correct mixture of ingredients. They knew that matter and spirit are not separate. Modern science is now revealing the same thing to us. Yet how the inner and outer worlds relate, and how our consciousness affects the physical world, remain for us still a great mystery.

Once we surrender our safe concept of a separate, static, and defined world, we open to a more dynamic reality in which life is an energy field with which our consciousness and unconscious interact: a pulsating Indra's Net being continually woven by the soul, through which our consciousness takes on form, our dreams come into being.

LIBERATING THE *ANIMA MUNDI*

We need the magical powers within nature in order to heal and transform our world. But awakening these powers would mean that our patriarchal institutions will lose their control, as once again the mysterious inner world will come into play, releasing forces once understood and used by the priestess and shaman, whose existence the patriarchal world has forgotten. The science of the future will work with these forces, exploring how the different worlds interrelate, including how the energies of the inner can be used in the outer. The shaman and the scientist will work together, the wisdom of the priestess and the wisdom of the physician renew their ancient connection.

But the first step is to awaken these powers, not just individually but for the whole world. We are moving into a global era, and any real changes need to be made globally. If we try to grasp powers for our own individual use, we risk descending into black magic, which is the use of inner powers for the purposes of the ego. Our next step in evolution is to realize the primal truth of oneness and to reunite our individual light with the whole.

The work pioneered by Jung has given us access to the science of alchemy, revealing this hidden part of our Western esoteric tradition. Psychological techniques have been developed to help reveal an inner world of energy, power, and creative potential. We no longer need to stay locked in the surface world. But our tendency has been to take this access for our individual selves, our own inner journey, and not realize its larger implications.

Real alchemical work was always for the sake of the whole. In our inner journey, our own alchemical process, to work for the sake of the whole means to acknowledge the dimension of the *anima mundi*. The light we discover in our own depths is a spark of the World Soul, and the world needs this light in order to evolve. When we make this connection in our consciousness and our imagination, we begin to change the fabric of life. The alchemists knew the potency of this spark, this philosophical mercury. The same substance that transforms our individual self is the primordial world-creating spirit, the "universal and scintillating fire in the light of nature, which carries the heavenly spirit with it." When we liberate it within ourselves but do not claim it just for ourselves, solely for our own inner process, we create certain connections through which this energy can flow into the core of life. We participate in the alchemical work of liberating the *anima mundi*. This is the first step in the work.

What does it really mean, to liberate the *anima mundi?* In our individual alchemical *opus* we experience the effects of freeing the light, energy, and creative potential that lie within us. We know how this liberation can radically change our vision and experience of life. We are taken into a different dimension of our self, and life begins to magically open doors that before were closed or hidden. Of course these changes are not always what we may want—they do not fulfill our surface desires, but they have a deeper meaning and purpose. Something within us awakens and the life of the spirit begins. The alchemists understood that the individual is a microcosm of the whole, and that what can happen to each of us can happen to the world.

When the light of the soul returns, a gray world of drudgery begins to sparkle; the multihued qualities of creation become visible. Instead of the endless pursuit of pleasure, life beckons us on a search for meaning: the colors of life speak to us, telling us their story, singing to us their song. The music of life returns, a music that *is* creation alive. A real dialogue between our inner self and our outer life begins to unfold as we directly participate in the hidden mystery of life coming alive: it comes alive within ourself and within the world. In the light of the soul the barriers between inner and outer dissolve, and we no longer have to dig beneath the surface for some semblance of purpose to our lives.

The light of the soul returning to the *anima mundi* will free us from the stranglehold of materialism, because it will awaken us to different qualities within life, give us different dreams to follow. In this light we will see life differently; a different world will become visible. When matter is dead and the soul is asleep, we are easily seduced by the addictions of materialism: we see nothing else to fulfill us. But we know in our own journey how we can suddenly be awakened to a different reality that was always around us and yet hidden from sight, a world that does not belong to buying and selling but to the mystery of the soul. Then a sense of wonder and awe returns. The same can happen with the world. We are longing to participate in a life that is multidimensional and full of beauty rather than just pursuing our own pleasure. Who would not turn from lust to love? The light of the soul is the spirit within matter that makes life dance. It awakens us to the simple joy of what is:

> i thank You God for most this amazing
> day:for the leaping greenly spirits of trees
> and a blue true dream of sky;and for everything
> which is natural which is infinite which is yes
>
> (i who have died am alive again today,
> and this is the sun's birthday;this is the birth
> day of life and of love and wings:and of the gay
> great happening illimitably earth)[19]

This is the world into which we were born. Even our city streets and shopping malls are alive in a way that is presently veiled. Creation is sparkling in so many ways, though its spectrum of colors is at present only partly visible. We have created a prison of materialism, but it is just an illusion. If we let life speak to us, it will show us the way to unlock this door, pull down these walls, dissolve this nightmare. There are forces within life more powerful than our corporations and politicians. And these forces do not play by the rules we have created. With laughter and a glint of mischief, they can rearrange our lives.

Our world is presently asleep. Its magical powers are for the most part dormant, but they are present, waiting to be used to transform our world. We have confined miracles to the safety of small events, but the whole world is miraculous. We may talk about the "miracle of life," but we place this miracle within the safe container of what we expect to happen. We do not dare to recognize that a real miracle is the unexpected, the Divine waking up in life. We may try to block off this dimension that is pure joy and light, to remain within the confines of our egos and expectations. But to do that is to deny the sacred nature of creation, deny that there is an Intelligence continually recreating the world according to divine principles that are beyond our rational understanding.

On our individual inner journey we begin to glimpse the workings of our soul, how it helps to create our outer life in an often miraculous way, as well as rearranging our inner selves. As we turn away from the ego towards the soul, we see more of its power and purpose. Its light is the ordering principle in our lives; it can create harmony out of the disparate aspects of our psyche, bring the mandala of the Self into being. Through the workings of the soul we begin to have an outer life in balance with our inner self. It is no different for the world. The *anima mundi* is the ordering and creative principle in creation. Without Her presence we experience only the fractious elements of our egos—the greed, insecurity, fears, and power dynamics that are so visible in our contemporary landscape. When Her light is awakened, then She can bring the world into harmony and balance. This simple and radical truth was known to the alchemists: it is the light hidden in matter that will redeem the world. That is why there is such a vital need to reconnect with the light of the sacred within each of us and within the Earth.

THE LIGHT OF
THE HEART

The Sun of His Light has risen in the hearts.
It shines, and for it there is no setting.

al-Hakîm at-Tirmidhî[1]

SPIRITUAL KNOWLEDGE OF THE HEART

This book tells the story of many connections, of stepping out of the insularity of our individual self into the
multidimensional reality that is all around us, with all
of its patterns of interconnection. As we begin to return
to our natural connection with the Earth, there are also
the connections between the worlds, and of reconnecting with the World Soul, with the light of the sacred
within creation. And the simplest and most direct way
to make these connections, to reconnect with the divine
oneness that is all around us, is through the heart. Not
the physical heart that pumps blood around our body,
but the spiritual heart through which love comes into
our life and into the world.[2]

Love is something so simple and mysterious, a feeling, a power, a vibration. It is the essence of our being,
the energy behind everything that exists. And yet it is

so subtle it is difficult to describe. We know when love is absent, a lack of warmth, a gray bleakness, life loses some essential substance, some color. But to describe love is more difficult. Is it passion, kindness, care, the tenderness of touch? It is not just a feeling, but an energy that draws us into a deeper connection with others and with the Divine. And it is a power that turns our heart towards the light, that can heal and transform. Real love is freedom and oneness and belonging, and it is found within the heart.

Love is the simplest essence of life and we need its consciousness and power for individual and global transformation. The center of this transformative consciousness is in the heart. If we are to live our spiritual potential and participate fully at this time of transition, we need to understand the mystical science of the heart. Then we can learn to use this spiritual organ as a means for global healing and awakening.

The human heart is a multidimensional organ of spiritual awareness and light. And as the human being is a microcosm of the whole of creation, the world itself has a heart of spiritual awareness and light. At its core, the human heart is one with the heart of the world, making our individual heart a doorway to the love and divine mystery of the whole. As we enter the chambers of our heart, we can access and work with the divine consciousness of the world. We can learn to live the love that holds the worlds together.

The mysteries of love, the science of the heart, have been revealed throughout the centuries in the esoteric knowledge of various mystical traditions. In particular, Sufism has made an extensive study of the human heart and its spiritual nature, expanding on how the spiritual organ within the heart transforms and awakens the wayfarer, leading to a more complete spiritual awareness, a deepening immersion in the light of the Divine until all traces of separation dissolve, "like sugar in water." Sufi wayfarers have mapped this journey into the inner, showing how the awakening of the heart's spiritual centers expands our consciousness, taking us from the limited horizon of our own self into the infinite ocean of divine love—that shoreless sea where "swimming ends always in drowning."

Much of this knowledge of the spiritual nature of the heart focuses on this interior journey of the wayfarer. However, there is another dimension of the science of the heart that until now has been kept hidden. This is how the heart of the individual can interact spiritually with the whole of life—the connection between our heart and the heart of the world. Within the heart, all the different levels of reality are connected together and here the inner flows directly into the outer.

Critical to this new dimension of our awareness is the recognition of how the human being is a microcosm of the whole. As we begin to understand this relationship, our sense of spiritual life and how we can be of service will change. We can recognize how our love can help heal and transform the Earth. This is an essential part of real spiritual activism.

THE INDIVIDUAL AS MICROCOSM

This knowledge which belongs to the coming era reflects how the individual functions as a microcosm of the whole and how the heart works as the direct spiritual connection between the individual and the whole. Man's pivotal position as a microcosm of creation can be found in Western spirituality in the tradition of alchemy. For the alchemists, man is "an image of the great world, and is called the microcosm or little world."[3]

In Sufism every human being is "made in the image of God." Ibn 'Arabî describes how the *hadîth* "God created Adam upon His own form" holds both for the great Adam, who is the cosmos in its entirety, and for the small Adam, who is the human being, and who is the microcosm. He explains:

> "He placed within man every one of His attributes, just as He placed all of His attributes within the cosmos." And the three basic worlds of the macrocosm—the spiritual, imaginal, and corporeal—are represented in man by the spirit (*rûh*), soul (*nafs*), and body (*jism*).[4]

Part of the esoteric significance of the relationship of macrocosm and microcosm is how the spiritual centers within the individual correspond to the whole of creation, its spiritual as well as physical body. In order to explore this relationship we need to recognize that the Earth as a whole is a living spiritual body. Then we can understand the relationship of microcosm and macrocosm as belonging not only to the exterior physical world, but to all of the worlds, "spiritual, imaginal, and corporeal," and we can see how an individual's spiritual centers, in particular the heart and its chambers, are central to this relationship.

The heart is a doorway between different levels of reality, existing in the physical world as well as in the soul's realm of pure love. The heart of an awakened human being has direct access to the heart of the world. If we think of ourself as separate from the whole of creation, we are not able to claim this connection, this inner affinity. But when we are awake to the oneness of which we are all a part, then this connection comes alive and the heart can function as a dynamic spiritual center in which different levels of reality are aligned together.

This alignment enables the individual to directly affect the whole in the same way that the heart affects the whole human being. When we feel divine love within the heart, the whole body rejoices. Nothing is excluded as the whole human being is directly nourished by the pure substance of divine love. As we come to understand the correspondence between the heart of the individual and the heart of the world, we will begin to unveil the mysteries of how an awakened heart can directly affect the Earth, and how this connection of the heart can be used to benefit life—how we can help love flow into life.

CHAMBERS OF THE HEART

The heart is the spiritual center of the human being. It is the home of the Self, our divine nature. "That Person in the heart, no bigger than a thumb, is known as maker of past and future.... That is Self."[5]

As the home of the Self, the heart is where our spiritual life unfolds, where we open to the inner reality of life and perceive the real meaning of the outer world. It is also in the heart that the microcosm and macrocosm meet. Through the heart we can perceive the infinite nature of our real Self, which is both individual and universal. The Self *is* the whole and thus within the heart we have direct access to the whole.

The heart is also where the energy structure of the Earth and the energy structure, or spiritual body, of the individual directly meet. It is through the heart that we can work most efficiently with the spiritual body of the

Earth, just as through the heart we can work most efficiently with our own spiritual body.

How do we work with the heart for the sake of the whole? How can we use the heart as a way of helping the spiritual evolution of the Earth? The simplest answer is love. Our love for the Earth, for this suffering being that has given us life, connects our heart and the heart of the world. Through this connection, healing and transformative divine power can flow simply and directly to where it is needed.

As some schools of Sufism have explored, there are different chambers or spiritual centers within the heart, each center corresponding to different dimensions of the inner world and to different levels of spiritual consciousness.

As early as the ninth century, al-Hakîm at-Tirmidhî wrote *A Treatise on the Heart*, in which he differentiated between four chambers of the heart: the breast (*sadr*), the heart (*qalb*), the inner heart (*fu'âd*), and the intellect (*lubb*). At-Tirmidhî describes the different qualities of spiritual awareness—the different lights—which belong to each chamber, with the innermost chamber having "the light of unification and the light of the contemplation of the uniqueness of God."[6]

Over the centuries Sufi teaching developed its study of the esoteric nature of the spiritual heart and explored how the heart functions within the spiritual development of the individual. In the ninth century Junayd cultivated the concept of the *latâ'if*, or subtle spiritual centers or organs of knowledge within the heart.[7] Later Sufi masters developed an understanding of the *latâ'if* as five centers or receptors of divine energy that come from more subtle cosmic realms.[8] Part of the spiritual science of the *latâ'if* is that these different spiritual centers within the heart correspond to different dimensions of the inner world; by activating a specific center, or *latîfah*, the wayfarer can travel in the corresponding interior realm.

Sufi masters developed practices and meditations to work with the energy of the heart, using different *dhikrs* and meditations for the different *latâ'if*. Traditionally the practitioner would progress gradually from one level to another over the course of his spiritual life. Each *latîfah* would open him to a different level of reality, and to the light and spiritual energy that belong to that level.

Part of the development of each level is learning to work with its energy so that it flows throughout the human being, bringing light and love where they are needed, helping the wayfarer to evolve. Finally, within the heart of hearts, all distinctions between lover and Beloved dissolve, and there is only divine light shining through the human being.

NOURISHING THE WORLD

There is a mystical science of how the heart of an awakened individual can be aligned with the energy structure of the Earth and be used to awaken and nourish life. While the mystical journey appears to be a turning away from the world, it actually embraces life in its innermost essence. From this central position the mystic can most directly help life change and evolve. The mystic has always played this role, but for millennia it has been veiled, often hidden even from the spiritual practitioner.

The heart is at the center of the human being and therefore at the center of life. Because the heart is a microcosm of the whole, it can speak directly to the Soul of the World. It can help clear the debris that is covering the world, and help the world be cleansed by love so that it shines more brightly and radiantly. An awakened heart can be used to help free life from negative patterns and attitudes.

Central to this science is that the heart naturally functions within the plane of unity, the dimension of the Self. In this dimension of oneness, to which the heart gives us access, everything is present in each moment and there are no constrictions of time and space. This means that within the heart we are free to be where we are needed. Love can flow directly from the Source—our inner light can go directly where it can be of service to life in the inner and outer worlds, not hindered by the darkness of the physical world. This potential is reflected in spiritual practices of global healing, in which one places the entire world within one's heart and nourishes it with one's light and love. If needed, one can then consciously direct one's attention and love to places of darkness or suffering, to where there is war or famine.

Once we acknowledge the relationship of macrocosm and microcosm within the oneness of life, it becomes apparent how our forgetfulness, our attitudes and actions, have caused pain to the Soul of the World. Our continued exploitation and greed has damaged the inner structures of light and love that nourish our planet; we have created dark clouds in the inner worlds that obscure us from the light. Our values are having a global effect, not only to our physical ecosystem but to the spiritual body of the Earth.

We are only beginning to take responsibility for the effects of our actions in the outer, physical world, but many people feel the damage that has been caused in the inner—feeling a loss of faith, a loss of joy and hope, a deep grief—and not knowing its cause. The Soul of the

World is crying out to be saved. It is the responsibility of spiritually awake human beings to hear and respond to this cry—to allow our hearts to be used for this work. We know how central love is to our own life, how it nourishes us in our very depths. A mother's love for her child is something fundamental to life. Their bond creates a sense of belonging and a quality of security that can last throughout life. Through the light and warmth of love we grow and expand and are able to realize our true potential as human beings. Love helps us to evolve through all the stages of life, from childhood to partnerships and parenthood.

One of the wonders of spiritual life is how we can be loved directly from the Source, experiencing divine love within the heart. This is a love that is not caught in any pattern of relationship or the dynamics of projection. It is pure love that flows into the heart from the inner planes. It comes through the chambers of the heart, directly connecting lover and Beloved, nourishing us in ways beyond our imaginings. It opens us to the reality of divine presence and awakens us to the real purpose of our life. It also transforms us, activating spiritual energy centers and our higher centers of consciousness.

What is true for the individual is true for the whole of creation. "In the whole of the universe there are only Two: the Lover and the Beloved. God loves His Creation, and the Soul loves God."[9] Through the heart this link of love can nourish all levels of life. Sometimes we experience this directly, as a sweetness or energy of love flows through our heart to a person we are with. But love flows through an awakened heart to all of creation, to the trees and the grass and stones and rivers—because everything is hungry for love. The whole of the world is a lover waiting for the Beloved.

This is the most beautiful conversation of life, the love that flows through everything, speaking of the real mystery of creation. The trees speak to the wind, to the birds and the rain, just as the Sun speaks to all of us. It speaks of the great belonging, to the Source, to the soul. Nothing is excluded, because in love there is no "other."

Love comes into the physical world, spinning the atoms of creation with the remembrance of God. Love also comes from the Source into the inner realms, into the imaginal or archetypal world of life's primal energies, and into the world of the soul.[10] The archetypes, the gods of the ancient world, need our love and attention, as some schools of psychology are now recognizing. These primordial forces that are the foundation of life respond to love, sometimes turning from resentful, angry beings into helpful and supportive forces, as is imaged in many fairy tales and tribal stories.

Love can free the archetypes of negative patterns and blocks that restrict the beneficial flow of their energy. Shamans traditionally work in the archetypal or imaginal world, and know the importance of relating to these forces with attention, respect, and love. Because love is such a powerful transformative force, it can directly affect these inner energies, enabling them to awaken to a higher and more creative potential.

For many years I worked in the inner world directly with the archetypes and witnessed the changes that love and attention can bring. I saw how empty barren inner landscapes could be planted with seeds of hope, which were tended with love, and how the landscape then became an orchard with fruit that nourished the soul and brought joy to life. I met a woman whose tears had blinded her eyes, so she could not see or look after her children. Through love she began to see and heal, and her children were no longer abandoned. Love brought healing and magic to the inner world, and the song of the future became alive. The child with stars in her eyes came to greet me, and showed me the dawn that was waiting for humanity. I saw a new prayer being given, which was also a seed opening to the Sun. Love can heal the inner world that has been abused by centuries of rationalism and forgetfulness.

Love can also directly heal the soul. Through love we can speak to the soul of another person, not just to the ego or personality. There are ancient ways to welcome the soul of a newborn child into the world, rituals of the heart that allow the infant not to forget her true nature so that the bond between soul and ego is not clouded or severed by the experiences of life, but nourishes the person throughout life.

And the heart can speak to the soul of an adult, healing wounds that the ego's or our culture's forgetfulness have inflicted. Some souls have been wounded by events in their life, by tragedy, heartbreak, or acts that caused suffering to others. Through the heart, light can be given to lift the dark clouds that surround such a soul, a darkness that is often experienced as depression. Because meaning comes from the inner, when our soul is veiled by such darkness life can become meaningless: we have lost the light of the soul. Love can restore it.

THE WORK OF THE LOVER

Working with love means that we respond from the core of our being to our global predicament. We can no longer afford to be isolated within our own spiritual practices or individual lives. At this time we are each called to make a commitment to the life of the Earth. Some are called to help heal Her body, to stop the toxins that are killing Her, destroying Her species and wild places. And some of us are drawn deeper, to help to heal Her soul, to bring light and love into the core of Her being. Our prayers, our attention, our loving are more powerful than we know.

How does the heart know how to respond? The wonder of the heart is that because it contains our higher spiritual intelligence, it instinctively knows where its attention and love are needed. The heart opens in response to a call. And the heart can differentiate types of need, just as a mother knows when the cry of her child is a cry of real pain or just a demand for attention.

Through the different chambers of the heart love works on different levels, from the outer physical world to the innermost where life's deepest secret is hidden. Through these different vehicles of love, the lover can bring love where it is needed, helping to heal a wounded Earth and also to activate energy centers that are dormant within the world. The lover has tasted the transformative nature of divine love, and knows its potential. *What can be given to the individual can be given to the world.* This is one of the secrets of global unity, of the emerging state of global awareness.

In our individual prayers, meditation, and devotions we work to be inwardly attentive and to align ourself with the Source. Mindfulness can bring us into the present moment, where we can respond to life's calling. Awareness of the breath is another way to align with the Source, as we attune ourself to the basic rhythm of life, our awareness flowing on the out-breath from the inner world of the soul into manifestation, and on the in-breath returning to the Source. A *dhikr* or *mantra* is another practice of inner alignment, as our consciousness is attuned to a divine name and That which it names. Another practice, already mentioned, begins a meditation or prayer by placing the world within the heart, reminding us of the all-inclusive nature of our practice.

What matters is a return to love. Because the world is created from love it responds most directly to love. Our culture limits love to the personal, but the Earth needs our hearts as well as our hands to help it to heal. We need to reclaim the mystery of our love for the Earth, this link within the heart that connects us directly to the heart of the world and to all of creation. We may feel this when we work in our garden, planting seeds with love, watching them grow with care, watering, and compost. Or we may sense it when we pick a wounded bird from the ground and help it to fly. Or just to stop for a moment and watch the clouds in the sky, sometimes rain comes, and sometimes sunshine. Simple acts of praise and thanksgiving as were known to our ancestors are a way to help love to flow into the world.

SPIRITUAL GROUPS

A spiritual group can be a powerful and beneficial organism of light and love in the world. Spiritual energy can be transmitted to the world through a group or a spiritual tradition. A group that meets regularly for spiritual practice has a group heart that sustains the group and also functions as a vehicle for spiritual energy. The efficiency of this spiritual organ depends upon the sincerity of the group, the level of development of its participants, and whether they are under the protection and guidance of a spiritual teacher. These factors also determine the level of energy to which they have access. The members of a group help each other on their individual journeys, but, bonded by their devotion and a shared spiritual purpose, they can also be used for the work of the whole. Every group has a different vibration, which determines the level of its participation and where it has access in the outer and inner worlds. Some groups or communities serve in the outer worlds, helping with healing or to improve the physical or social conditions of people's lives. Other groups work close to the physical world, helping to heal the etheric body of the Earth, while other groups may work in the archetypal or angelic worlds, and still others work deep in the inner, even in the planes of non-being.

Spiritual groups form part of the spiritual body of the Earth, its body of light. Seen from this perspective, the groups are not separate, independent entities, but part of an organic, living being. They are formed where they are needed by the spiritual body of the Earth, where their love and light need to constellate. Throughout the history of the Earth, spiritual energy and activity have focused in different physical locations. In more recent centuries India and Tibet have been the locality of much spiritual work, while the flowering of Sufism in the earlier part of the millennium points to a spiritual focus in the Middle East, although Genghis Khan and his Mogul warriors brought devastation to much of that region, causing many Sufis to migrate west to Damascus and Anatolia. In recent years many different traditions have moved from the East to the West, which appears to be the present focus of much spiritual energy and activity.

As a living, spiritual being, the Earth changes, its focus of light moves, and the spiritual work that is done by practitioners changes. Our focus on the individual dimension of spiritual work often overlooks this larger, global picture; it misses the way spiritual groups and their work are all interrelated. Sadly, many present-day practitioners remain isolated within the image of their own path as something separate, rather than embracing a vision of dynamic wholeness in which each practitioner is like a different cell in the light body of the Earth, not recognizing how the different spiritual paths and traditions are just different ways of working with the one light.

It is only when we are working together that we can overcome many of the present obstacles created by global consumerism and the desecration it inflicts on the planet. When the different paths are linked together in the inner and outer worlds, they will realize their real transformative potential and help the world awaken.

Much spiritual work is veiled, hidden in the inner worlds. But sometimes we are given a glimpse of the nature of this work, in particular the work of the masters of wisdom who look after the spiritual well-being of the planet. A friend had the following vision, which images some of the work of the Naqshbandi Sufi order, guided by the presence of its founder, the thirteenth-century master 'Abd'l-Khâliq Ghijduwânî:

> During the meditation I found myself, after a short journey of the soul away from the earth, in a gigantic space station outside of our galaxy in the universe. Suddenly I found myself in a control room standing to the right of Sheikh Ghijduwânî. Around us there were only shining and blinking computers and control panels.
>
> Through the windows I could see, below us to the right, our galaxy, with the beautiful earth against a black background. I also saw energy- and light-canals which reached to other galaxies.

Sheikh Ghijduwânî explained much to me about his current work. Some of it I could hold on to.

He said he now creates connections on various levels of reality to other living galaxies so that there can be a connection between them and ours. Various dark powers endlessly try to hinder this. However, they do not succeed, since divine evolution and the power of love and surrender of the masters are stronger. Saying this, he laughed deeply and cheerily.

Then I looked to our beautiful brightly shining planet, which was enclosed in gray and black zones like fog. Through the fog an energy spiral spun very fast, on various levels of existence. At the same time I recognized this spiral as the energy field of our Sufi order. This spiral, fed through the love and surrender of meditators, slowly dissolves this fog of divine forgetting and of darkness on various levels of existence.

The master said he was working at this place in the universe in order to balance out certain energies between the galaxies, and to protect these galaxies, including our own. He works always under order from the Almighty.

He doesn't work alone; he works also with Buddhist teachers and masters.

This vision takes the friend away from the Earth to where a vaster dimension of spiritual work is revealed, work that is creating "connections on various levels of reality to other living galaxies." Just as connections and patterns of relationship are being created in our world as different groups and spiritual traditions are being linked together, other connections and relationships are being formed in the vaster macrocosm. Then the vision shows the work of the masters of love in this world, creating an energy field that dissolves the fog of forgetfulness and darkness that covers our planet. This energy field, "fed through the love and surrender of meditators," is "on various levels of existence," because the fog of forgetfulness and the darkness that need to be dissolved also exist on different levels. Our culture has created pollution and darkness far into the inner worlds. An important aspect of real spiritual work is its ability to function on different levels, to work in the subtle, inner worlds. The different centers within the heart give us access to different levels of reality, and through the guidance of the masters we work together to bring the energy of the path where it is needed.

In its final statement, the vision shows that the different paths are not working in isolation: "He doesn't work alone; he works also with Buddhist teachers and masters." The coming era is one of cooperation and interrelationship. Within the heart everything is one. Just as the heart can reconnect an individual with the unity inherent within her, so can it connect us with the unity of all life. When we bring this consciousness into life, we recognize that we are all working together for the sake of the whole, we are each part of a living organism that needs our care and attention.

There is a vast spectrum of love, from caring for a child, caressing our partner's body, tending a plant in the garden, to bringing an energy of healing into the flow of life. All around love is calling to us, in the tender places of our hearts, in our dreams, and in the endless waves falling onto the shoreline. We hold the stories of love in our hearts, our own need for love and our giving. If we can pause for a moment and in the stillness hear the cry of the Earth we will know to give a place in our hearts to this beautiful, suffering being. Our open heart may bring us tears, a taste of the deep sorrow of this time, but we may also feel a spark within the heart of the world. The light of our love is our simplest and most valuable gift.

THE AXIS OF LOVE

*Love is the principle of existence
and its cause;
it is the beginning of the world
and what maintains it.*

Ibn 'Arabî[1]

THE WORLD SPINS ON AN AXIS OF LOVE

The axis of love runs through creation, carrying the energy of love to every atom. It belongs to the spiritual core of the Earth and brings color to all the different hues and variations of love that give meaning and beauty to life. Without it there would be no joy, no hope, no love present in the world.

The axis of love sings the song of creation, the joy and wonder that are central to all of life. It is a direct expression of the divine love affair that underlies all of existence. We are all an expression of divine love, and this gravitational pull of love holds life together; it gives sustenance to all of creation.

The axis of love belongs to the spiritual structure of the Earth. It spins at a very high frequency, which makes it almost invisible even to the inner eye, but it is a very powerful core of energy that nourishes life more than we realize. Like the magnetic core of the Earth, the axis of love also creates an energetic field that protects our Earth from forces of darkness. And it speaks to the heart of every seeker who turns towards the Divine, reminding us of our true nature and of the love that is in the core of our being. In a more diffuse way it nourishes all of creation, connecting each atom to the Source, to the bond of love between the Creator and the creation.

It is part of the wonder of the way the world is created that this axis of love is present in every grain of sand, every drop of rain, every laugh, every tear. But the density of the world limits the flow of divine love through it. Human darkness, cruelty, greed, and corruption add to the density, creating negative energy fields that can be clearly seen on the inner planes. Thus the natural flow of love and light that should nourish life in the inner and outer worlds has become partly blocked. The spread of materialistic values that deny the sacredness of the Earth has intensified this problem and made it global. There are very few places left where the energy can flow freely, just as there are few places in the physical world that remain unpolluted. The collective attitude of humanity has a powerful effect on the inner nourishment of the world.

Because the heart of the mystic belongs to her Beloved, she can bypass many of the patterns of resistance that block the flow of love and light around the world. The axis of love is most directly accessible through the heart, because the heart is our organ of divine perception and divine love. Through the heart we are aligned with the center of our being and with the axis of love that runs through creation. Through the awakened hearts of lovers, divine love can flow directly into the world and here the axis of love is consciously present—it is not veiled as in the hearts of those who follow their own desires, who know only the dimension of their own ego-self. Lovers carry the consciousness of the divine love affair that is the essence of life, and in their remembrance and daily life they live this love affair. They are the people of love. The work of the Sufis and other lovers of God has always been to keep the axis of love pure and protected, so that the world spins on it without distortion, so that divine love flows into creation. Through our prayers, our practices, and the openness of our heart, we are present at the axis of love. Our love for God, the love between lover and Beloved, sings along it. In this way we live it in this world.

The lover looks after the axis of love in the world through the simplicity of her devotions, through keeping her heart pure and the attention of the heart turned towards the Divine while she lives her everyday life. How we live the love affair that is creation is unique to each of us. No two ways of love are the same. But every lover lives the same axis of love. It is alive in our hearts, present in each and every breath. And when we remember our Beloved, it sings within us, nourishing life in the most hidden and wonderful ways.

Everything in life is a lover waiting for its Beloved, longing to return to the Source. Just as love draws human lovers together, it draws everything back to union. If there were no love holding creation together, everything would fall apart. Every molecule is part of a play of love and longing that hides and reveals Her face. We fulfill our part in this love affair in the simplest of ways—through relating to others with loving kindness, through cooking or cleaning with love, through living our daily life with remembrance and awareness, which for the Sufi is the awareness of the heart.

Through this awareness we recognize our Beloved in the world; we feel love's presence in the beauty and the chaos: in a summer sunrise as well as in the rush-hour traffic. Love is within us and within everything we meet: it is in the noise of the alarm clock and the taste of the toast. When we remember with our heart, when we bring this awareness into our daily life, we are the note of love in the world. Our hearts form part of the spinning axis of divine love. Our work is to live this axis of love, and to keep it pure, just as we keep our heart pure and polished.

There are many distractions that can take us away from this work of love. Our psyche offers us endless problems; the world holds so many seductions and distortions. And in our culture we think of love as something special, a privilege that some are born into through the gift of a loving parent. We hunt for love in relationships, seek it in friendship or love affairs. We try to give it to our children. We package our idea of love in hopes and disappointments, fears, anxieties, and self-judgments. We enclose it in our psychological problems.

We can follow the discord within us, our lack of self-worth, our jealousies and anger. We can project love outside ourselves and run after the ego's fantasies and desires. Or we can acknowledge the ordinariness of love; we can recognize that love is the primal substance of creation, a basic energy within all of life. Then we can find the thread of love within ourself and within our everyday life, and begin to see the many ways divine love expresses itself.

Once we look carefully, with attention and presence, we can find love everywhere—"wheresoever you turn there is the face of God." And through the simplicity of our own awareness, we can weave this thread of love into the fabric of our days.[2] We can bring a knowing of love into the outer world which is starving for real nourishment.

When we awaken to the presence of love and begin to relate to all life as a way to love God, then something opens within the human being and we can participate in this mystery of love in the most ordinary everyday things. Opening a car door, picking up a bag of groceries with love and remembrance, we are directly interacting with this love affair of creation. We are breathing with the breath of God, loving with the love of God in everything we do. In this way we carry the knowing of God's love for the world, and help life come alive with this note of love.

Divine love is not always sweet; often it is bitter, sometimes even mundane. It is simple and so easily overlooked. It is a way to relate to life, a way to recognize what is real, a way to remember the sacred. And once we glimpse this love, it needs our constant attention; it needs the work of a heart attuned to love. The path prepares us for this work. It attunes our heart to the frequency of divine love. The practices of the path transform the heart so that we can awaken within love. Then we need to live it fully, to "give it blood." This is the remembrance of the heart lived in every breath, in every act. This is our mystical contribution to life, the song of our soul as an offering of love.

A NEW NOTE OF DIVINE LOVE

The love at the axis of the world has a vibration or musical note that is central to the mystery of revelation—the way the world reflects its Creator. The world is a place of divine revelation, and this note attunes creation to the mystery of divine love.

This revelation is not static, but a continually evolving dance of lover and Beloved who: "never reveals Himself in the same form twice." The divine revelation changes every moment, in each new bud on every tree, in every bird flying across the sky. There are also patterns of revelation; the ways that divine self-disclosure changes with each new age. This is why every age has its own particular signs of God, and why between the ages there can be a period of confusion and transition as the old signs no longer hold meaning and the new signs are not yet recognized.[3]

We are currently in such a time of transition. A new note is waiting now to be infused into creation, to be brought into the axis of love and from there into the whole tapestry of life, the interconnected web of creation. The new note will help align creation with the patterns of revelation that belong to the coming age, and will carry a new vibration that will affect life in a slightly new way.

We have forgotten that spiritual consciousness, like all life, evolves. The note of love in the previous era helped point us to a monotheistic divinity beyond our physical world. A transcendent God was the gift of the patriarchal era, which was marked by a perception of duality: earth and heaven, matter and spirit. Spiritual practices and teachings worked within the context of this understanding, guiding us further and further away from the Earth and instinctual life, while knowledge about the physical world was left to the discoveries of science.

Part of the new pattern of revelation is a celebration of divine oneness and the sanctity of divine presence. The note of love of the coming era has the potential of awakening humanity to the divine oneness within all life. The different levels and dimensions of reality will reflect this oneness in a new way. For example, instead of understanding levels of reality as hierarchical, a ladder of spiritual ascent, we will be able to experience all levels as integral parts of a multidimensional whole—nothing is higher or lower in oneness. Since love is everywhere, this new vibration will be able to go to places that have long been forgotten, releasing the light in the depths of matter, for example.

The new note of love is so new that we can hardly imagine what it will reveal. But it is like a key to a new perception. It can awaken centers of power and ways of spiritual perception both within the Earth and within humanity that will contribute to a whole new pattern of life, a new relationship between Creator and creation, a new way of living divine love.

Part of the work of mystics and lovers at this time is to help to bring it into life. While the heart of the mystic looks towards God, she is also present in life: we are a part of the world of creation as well as being awakened to the inner worlds of light and love. The mystic is part of the axis of love in the outer and inner worlds, the world of the senses and the world of light. The note of love that is present within our heart is also present in the cells of our body, and is thus brought into the world of creation.

Our physical self, our body and instinctual nature, is part of the web of life. It belongs to the interdependent living organism that is our Earth. We are all connected in both the inner and outer worlds, part of an organic unity. Through the heart of the mystic the new note of love is brought from the uncreated worlds into the worlds of creation where it is immediately part of life's oneness. The note that sings in the lover sings in all of life. Nothing is excluded.

Before the lover can bring this note into life, she has to be fully aligned with this new pattern. The hearts and also the consciousness of divine lovers have to be subtly changed. This work is taking place now. And this realigning happens not just individually but also on a group level:

groups of lovers as well as other types of spiritual seekers are being realigned, their inner and outer orientation changed. This is happening because it is through groups of individuals that the spiritual energy needed for the new unfolding can be most easily transmitted. Spiritual groups are the spiritual centers of the coming age.[4]

Realigning groups and individuals takes time. We all have our patterns of resistance, our identification with old ways. While the hearts of His lovers may be open, often our patterns of consciousness are more crystallized. Groups also have their patterns and spiritual identities that can become fixed.

The new note of love needs our conscious participation: we need to know that we are a dynamic part of an unfolding oneness that is also a new face of revelation. The new note of love needs also to be a knowing that we are one.

AWAKENING FROM A DREAM

This new note of love comes from the inner, uncreated worlds, the "dark silence" that is near to the Source. From this emptiness galaxies are born, as is the love that sustains them. Lovers and mystics who are inwardly immersed in the uncreated emptiness can have direct access to love that is not constricted by form. Their hearts are a space for this love to come into the world.

So much in the inner worlds is changing. For example, the archetypal structures of life are changing—the pure energy of creation is beginning to flow into new patterns, like water flowing along newly formed riverbeds. And in the plane of oneness, which is the dimension of the Self, human consciousness is becoming more awake to the dynamics of how oneness works. An awareness of global unity and the "interbeing" of life is beginning to enter our collective consciousness.

Changes are also taking place in the uncreated worlds, which contain the invisible forces behind creation. The dazzling darkness, the nothingness beyond the mind, is full of energy that has not yet manifested even into light. Many of the changes that we sense in our outer life—for example, newly developing patterns of relationship that function non-hierarchically—have their origins in deep changes taking place in this emptiness.

Just as love is born in the emptiness, so too are the new vibrations of love. A spiritual master who is immersed in these inner dimensions can attune the hearts of his disciples to these vibrations. Then the love that flows from master to disciple will have a slightly different vibration, which will affect the whole being of the disciple. Through the heart and physical body of the disciple this new vibration of love comes into being.

The axis of love is present in everything, just as the name of God is written on every cell of creation. But because this axis is most accessible in the hearts of lovers—those who have given their lives to divine love—it is through our hearts that we can bring this new note of love from love's source in the uncreated into life. From the innermost center of our heart, the secret of secrets to which only the Beloved and love's servants have access, the note of love comes into the world of creation, into our instinctual nature and physical body.

This note includes everything: there is no differentiation into light or dark, low or high. Everything is a celebration of love. It is the ability of the lover to bring together the innermost and the outer worlds, all bonded together in love and service, that allows the note of love to be transmitted without discord. The more completely the lover is surrendered in service, the more effortless is this work. When the whole being of the lover completely bows down in service and surrender, the note of love resonates effortlessly at its highest frequency.

It is important to include the physical, because the new note of love needs to be heard in the physical body of the Earth, in the places where our greed and ignorance have polluted and desecrated its wonder and beauty. This work with the physical belongs particularly to women, because it is through a woman's physical body and being that love flows most easily into the physical world. This is an aspect of the sacred mystery of motherhood, a woman's capacity to give birth. Unlike a man's, a woman's physical body contains the sacred substance of creation. Every woman carries in her cells a light, absent in men's bodies, that allows the light of a soul to take on form through her body, divine love to manifest physically in a new human being. This sacred substance and light that women uniquely carry will also allow the new vibration of love to reach into the physical body of the world.

Love is a language that most of us have forgotten.[5] We think of love as a warm fuzzy feeling, a sense of caring, or a passionate embrace. But love is the most direct connection between the Creator and Her creation. Love is how the Creator speaks most directly to the world, and it conveys both knowledge and nourishment. There are so many subtleties to love's language, which speaks to both our souls and our bodies. And part of its wonder is that it can flow through our hearts and into the world without diluting its ability to convey life's sacred meaning.

The new note of love is partly like an encoded message that will speak to creation, awakening it from the past era's nightmare of pollution and desecration. It will talk to the world about the patterns of oneness that exist within it, and the way the energy of life can flow along these patterns, cleansing and purifying the world. Life has been waiting to hear this secret message. Until it is heard, life cannot awaken. We have forgotten that divine love can speak to the world, just as we have long forgotten the sacred and magical connections to the world that exist within women. We have been living our rational dream of separation and isolation until it has become a soul-destroying nightmare.

Just as divine love awakens each of us, so it can awaken the world. Love turns the heart and gives us a knowing of what is real. In the light of divine love we discover our purpose and learn to live what is sacred within us. Without this touch of love we remain asleep, knowing only the dream world of the ego. In that dream we follow the cycles of suffering and desire, but when we awake we realize that another world is present around us, a world in which we are given what we need and are nourished by the primal joy of life. When the world awakes, its complex problems will soon dissolve like a bad dream, as we all realize that there is a way to relate through life's natural connections, through the oneness that is fundamental to all of us. And through these new organic patterns of relationship we will discover new economic and social structures that can nourish all of us, without damaging the web of life. The new era can be self-sustaining in ways we have yet to imagine.

LIVING LOVE'S NEW NOTE

What does it mean to be awake and receptive to this new note of love? The challenges will be different for each of us. But it will be helpful to remember that this note of divine love is *new*. It does not belong to the spiritual lexicons of the past. It brings together the worlds in a new way. It is a joy waiting to be lived, a new bud on the tree of life. It will touch us in ways that we have not been touched; it will awaken us within a world alive with divine presence.

Every part of life speaks to every other part in the language of love, and we can learn this language. We can learn once again how to talk to life and listen to life's response. We can see the patterns of love as they are present in life: the signs that the Beloved has placed in creation. We can learn to work with the magic and power of love within life—in the oneness that includes everything in the inner and outer worlds, not just in the secret inner spaces of the heart, in meditation or prayer.

To participate in these changes, we must leave behind any pattern of spiritual isolation that might separate us from life or from each other, or any image of hierarchical spiritual ascent. Our Beloved is not a solitary inner figure but a dynamic oneness that embraces the seen and unseen worlds. Living the wholeness of love means stepping outside any pattern of conditioning into an ever-expanding universe of the created and the uncreated. Patterns that restrict our unconditional openness to the oneness of life will limit our ability to live and transmit this love.

All we need to do is acknowledge that we are a part of life and a part of God. Our higher and lower natures contain the worlds. Every cell of our body, every touch of our hands, has the axis of love at its core and the patterns of creation in the way it moves. And the note of love communicates what is real to the whole; it helps to reveal our Beloved's face in the world.

Living the note of love will take us to the edge of ourselves, into the density of life and the light of the heart.

We will see how those things are part of each other, how the light needs the darkness and how we are that darkness. And we will sense that something new is coming into being, within us and within the world.

This is not a spiritual exercise but something that we have been waiting for. To be alive at the center of life in this moment of time is a blessing as we help the world throw off the dust of a thousand years. Traditionally Sufis are known as sweepers, sweeping up the dust of the world, and there is much work to be done!

We are sweeping away the dust of forgetfulness and the debris of the last patriarchal era. We are bringing the new note of love from the depths of our hearts into the thoroughfares of the world. And we are learning to look at life through the eye of the heart, a consciousness attuned to the new note of love that enables us to see love's revelation. In the midst of life our Beloved is unveiling Herself once again and this secret needs to be seen, love's hidden treasure needs to be known. Mystics are the eyes and ears of God and can read the book of life. But we need to be awake, to be fully alive in the present moment, in order to read the book of life as it is being written anew.

The book of life is our own life. The new note of love is being born in our own life, allowing us to see and experience our Beloved in a new way. A central core of this experience is the revelation of divine oneness in the midst of the world. Nothing is separate, nothing is excluded. Every breath is a divine breath. We can see life through the eyes of the ego, which tells its story of unfulfilled desires, isolation, and patterns of protection, or we can recognize that another story is being told in which our individual self is part of the whole of creation. This interconnected, living wonder includes the addict and his needle and the child and her new toy: we are the spider and its bite and the hummingbird and its taste of nectar. We are life in all its manifold expressions of the One. We are here to experience the fullness of life and know that it is God.

Every day, every moment, we have to say "Yes" to our Beloved and "Yes" to life. In this primal "Yes" we celebrate divine presence in our life and in the world. We are not here to change the world, but to experience it through the eyes of revelation. Then we will see that it has already changed, and what most people imagine as life is just the fading images of the previous era. Looking through the patterns of conditioning, we see a dying world destroying itself with greed and pollution. Through the eyes of revelation, we will see a new world forming amidst these shadows.

Through our unconditional "Yes" we claim our right to see with the light of the new, to experience what is being born. And then, in a moment both so simple and so extraordinary, we will realize that we are what is being born. In the miracle of divine oneness the center of life is within us; the mystery of life happens in every moment for each of us. We are the center of the circle. We are life's new revelation of love.

EPILOGUE

Half a century ago I first experienced the spark of love's oneness, connections of love and care that link us with each other, regardless of race or place. Over the years since, I have watched that spark struggle to come alive, to awaken us to the real meaning of global unity. I have sensed its promise for humanity and the whole Earth, a return to the song of the sacred as the foundation of life.

I have also witnessed the darkening cloud of our culture's false promise of prosperity, how it tears at the fragile web of life that supports us all. And now, all around us we see the debris of a dying civilization, one that has raped and pillaged its way across the Earth. And its destruction and desecration continue, as rainforests are clear-cut for cattle or palm oil, the oceans fill with plastic at a rate unfathomable a few decades ago, and species die out at an increasing rate, killed by our use of pesticide and loss of habitat. More subtle but just as poignant, is the loss of wild places and wonder, and the constant clamor of our world that denies us the silence needed to hear what is really present.

But the story of oneness has also grown more alive. Many of us are awakening, feeling the grief for what is being lost, and also articulating and living a new story, one based upon the deep knowing of our interconnection with all of the living Earth and Her many inhabitants. We are a part of the streams and the rivers and the rain and the trees, part of a multihued wonder that is crying out for our care and attention, that desperately needs our love. This new story is like a spring awakening in the dark days of a winter of separation, and yet still we are surrounded by the monster of materialism we have created, devastating our ravaged world.

So many voices call for us to act before it is too late, before the Earth warms and ecocide throws our world too far out of balance. And in the years since I first wrote about the story of oneness these voices have increased, offering different ways to transition to the future our hearts long for, when we embrace a way of life that is sustainable not just for humanity but all of creation; when we relearn the "Original Instructions" that the First Peoples have kept in trust. And yet in many of these offerings I have found a central ingredient missing, a catalyst for real change and transformation. *We cannot make this shift on our own.* We need the help, the love, the power, the deep knowing that comes from the inner worlds where grace is born. We have created this self-destructive imbalance because we forgot the deep roots of our being, the sacred nature of all that exists. As we imagined ourselves masters of the world, we dismissed the guidance and help that comes from within, from the Divine that is our very essence. We turned away from miracles and magic. We forgot what every culture before us knew: the Earth is a sacred being, and if we lose our connection to what is sacred, we cannot survive, we cannot grow and evolve together.

All those who have travelled on their own journey know this simple truth—how we need the healing, the love, the unconditional acceptance that comes with grace, with blessing. With our own weary feet we cannot find the way. And what is true for each of us is true for the Earth and all of us. We need the help that is waiting to be given. But first we have to open our hearts and minds and turn towards the Source. We need to reconnect with what is Real—the lover with the Beloved.

The Earth is a living spiritual being that is at present undergoing a painful time of transition, and we are here to help it transform. Human beings are able to be a connection between the worlds—the inner worlds of light and love and the outer physical world. And the Earth needs this connection. We can bring the light of the soul into the world. We can reconnect with the nature spirits, the *devas*, and the angels, and together help to heal our dying ecosystem. We are the link of love between the worlds.

This book is a story of the shift that is possible, of the awakening of the Earth, when the song of creation can be heard again and humanity find its place and balance in the wonder that is always around us. But it is also the story of the darkness and grief of this present time, of the danger that we do not take this step into the dawn. It describes some of the ancient ways that spiritual energy works in the world, in the physical body of the Earth and the inner worlds of light and love. And it suggests ways we can use this deep knowing at this present time, to reconnect the worlds so that love and light can flow and heal.

The new story of an awakening Earth is a story of oneness, the oneness of all of creation, which includes not only the webs of dew in an early summer morning, the laughter of children, the tears of lovers, but also all the subtle worlds, the spirits and angels, the names of God and the masters of wisdom. We are all part of a living, magical wholeness, bonded together in love. We are the vast ocean and the blade of grass. We are the drunkard staggering home at night and the child waiting for the school bus. And we are our own ordinary self, feeling better after a cup of coffee in the morning. And we are also the world waiting before dawn, tired of the darkness, needing the light of the souls of lovers to awaken.

In the light of love's oneness, life is as it has always been. Fruit grows on the fruit tree and is sold in the marketplace. The cycle of life continues. But something is different. Something is coming into being that was not here before—something is becoming visible that was hidden. What has changed, what is new? Something lovers know within their hearts is being given to the world. Part of love's secret self is being made visible. How this will change our world hangs in the balance.

We are here at a moment in time and we are this moment, each alive in our own way. Watch carefully and you can see what is being given, what is being passed from heart to heart. You can see the connections coming alive, reconnecting us to the living Earth and Her soul. Something new is being made known, and we are a part of it. We are a secret being reborn, a way of praise and prayer that includes all of creation, that is a celebration of divine oneness. And before the tide turns and this moment is gone, we need to plant the seed of this prayer into the depths of the Earth, into the places of power, into the currents of love that flow through the Earth. Then the world can awaken.

NOTES

OPENING PAGES

1. The other books in this series, published by The Golden Sufi Center, are: *The Signs of God* (published 2001), *Working with Oneness* (2002), *Light of Oneness* (2004), *Spiritual Power: How It Works* (2005, with second edition published in 2019), and *Alchemy of Light: Working with the Primal Energies of Life* (2007).
2. "The Mother Womb Creates the Human (Babylonian-Assyrian)," from *Desert Wisdom: A Nomad's Guide to Life's Big Questions from the Heart of the Native Middle East*, by Neil Douglas-Klotz, p. 24.

PREFACE TO NEW EDITION

1. *Aluna* is the Kogi name for the intelligence within nature, the thought process that shapes and maintains reality, the source of life.

   The Kogi are an Indigenous people living in the Sierra Nevada in Colombia, whose civilization has continued since the pre-Columbian era. Their priests, or Mamas, work together with *Aluna*, the spiritual intelligence within nature, to help to keep the world in balance. Since the 1990s they have given warnings to the "younger brothers" of the dangers of ecological imbalance, the potentially catastrophic future facing the planet if we don't change our ways.
2. The Network of Spiritual Progressives (https://spiritualprogressives.org/philosophy/spiritual-activism/). Subtle Activism, pioneered by Dr. David Nicols, refers to "the use of consciousness-based practices for collective transformation," and he has also formed a community called the Subtle Activism Network. Unity Earth is another community that links these ideas together, focusing on the simple truth "that we are one."
3. The phrase "inner world" refers to subtle states of consciousness that transcend the known physical universe. This concept may be found in religious, metaphysical, and esoteric teachings, which propound the idea of a whole series of subtle planes or worlds or dimensions which, from a center, interpenetrate themselves and the physical planet in which we live, the solar systems, and all the physical structures of the universe. This interpenetration of planes creates a multi-dimensional universe with many different levels of consciousness.

INTRODUCTION

1. "Original Instructions" are ancient ways of living from the heart of humanity within the heart of nature, the simple guidebook of how to be on this Earth, that we have to "get along together" with all of creation.

CH 1: THE FIRST STEP

1. It is present in the teachings of Christ, who was the light of the world, and there is evidence from the Gnostic gospels that early Christians were given access to this "blazing fire." But sadly by the fourth century the Christian Church chose worldly power over real spiritual transformation, the Gnostics were banned, and later groups like the Cathars were persecuted.
2. See the work of Peter Kingsley, www.peterkingsley.org.
3. *Gospel of Mark* 2:22.

CH 2: SPIRITUAL MATURITY AND SERVICE

1. Andrew Harvey, "Step by Step," *Light Upon Light: Inspirations from Rumi*, p. 112.
2. According to some researchers the build up of CO_2 and methane began much earlier, with the massive deforestation that had taken place over the world by two thousand years ago. Charles Eisenstein, *Climate: A New Story*, pp. 102–103.
3. Christian persecution of paganism was particularly intense during the reign of the Roman emperor Theodosius I (C.E. 392–395).
4. *Darkening of the Light: Witnessing the End of an Era*, by Llewellyn Vaughan-Lee, published in 2013 by The Golden Sufi Center.

CH 3: COLLIDING FORCES

1. "Her Triumph," *Collected Poems of W. B. Yeats*, p. 310.
2. "The Second Coming," *Collected Poems of W. B. Yeats*, p. 210.
3. Later, the empire founded by Ghengis Khan created an environment that encouraged trade, the exchange of ideas, and religious tolerance.
4. See Peter Kingsley, *Reality*, for a fuller exploration of *metis* in the teaching of the ancient Greeks.
5. The popularity of the *Harry Potter* series points to our longing for a world not restricted by the blindness of the "muggles."

CH 4: THE RELATIONSHIP BETWEEN THE WORLDS

1. *Spiritual Power: How It Works*, by Llewellyn Vaughan-Lee, first edition, 2005; revised second edition, 2019.
2. The use of the imagination to explore the symbolic world belongs both to alchemy and Sufism, see Vaughan-Lee, *Working with Oneness*, ch. 8: "Imagination"; and the spiritual energies of this inner realm are described by Henry Corbin in *Creative Imagination in the Sufism of Ibn 'Arabi*.
3. In *For Love of the Real: A Story of Life's Mystical Secret*, I explore the different interior worlds that belong to our mystical consciousness.

4. In Indian yoga the world of creation belongs to the first three centers of consciousness, or *chakras* (the root-, the sexual-, and the solar-plexus *chakras*), while the four higher centers (the heart-, the throat-, the brow-, and the crown *chakras*) belong to spiritual consciousness. Most people function with the three lower *chakras*, while the four higher centers are awakened through spiritual practice.

5. In yoga these energy drives are associated respectively with the three lower *chakras*.

6. First Epistle of Paul to the Corinthians 13:12.

7. The thirteenth-century Sufi, Najm al-Dîn Razî, describes how the world gives the soul, or spirit, a fuller experience of the Divine: "For in the beginning the spirit had knowledge of universals and not of the particulars; it had knowledge of the world of the unseen and not of the manifest. When it was joined to this world and duly trained and nurtured, it acquired knowledge of both universals and particulars, and became 'knower of the unseen and the manifest' as God's vicegerent." From *The Path of God's Bondsmen*, p. 363.

8. Two excerpts from *The Path of God's Bondsmen: From Origin to Return*, by Najm Al-Dîn Razî, trans. by Hamid Algar, p. 140n.

9. *Psalm* 36:9.

10. Bruce Lipton, "The Biology of Inspiration," *Healing the Heart of the World*, p. 332.

11. See the work of Peter Wohlleben, *The Hidden Life of Trees*.

12. The Findhorn Foundation of Scotland whose beautiful gardens were co-created with the nature *devas*, is an example of working together with the subtle forces within nature. The land was originally sand dunes, barren and dry, unsuited to anything other than hardy Scottish bushes and grasses requiring little moisture or nourishment.

    There are many different *devas* who are the custodians of the forces within nature. A friend who is descended from the Bushmen of the Kalahari, taught me how each species has its own *deva*, who carries the intelligence of the species, whether fox or deer, robin or crab. With the natural wisdom of his people he was able to inwardly communicate directly with these *devas*.

13. Shakespeare, *Hamlet* (1.5.167–8). Prince Hamlet is here specifically referring to the ghost of his dead father. But he is also describing his more ambiguous world of dreams and spirits, than the rational world of thought to which Horatio, as a man of reason, belongs (*ratio* is the Latin word for "reason").

14. It is always advised to have a guide or protector when entering the shamanic world. Unlike the angels, not all spirits and elemental beings are friendly, and their ways are often very unfamiliar to our Western consciousness. I have met people who became possessed by these spirits with negative consequences. One must walk carefully and with respect.

CH 5: ANIMA MUNDI: AWAKENING THE SOUL
OF THE WORLD

1. Stephan Hoeller, *Gnosis: A Journal of Western Inner Traditions*, vol. 8, Summer 1988.
2. Timaeus 30D3–31A1, *Plato's Timaeus*, trans. F. M. Cornford.
3. There is a tradition that medieval stained-glass makers were taught by alchemists how to use glass to transform light.
4. David Fideler, *Restoring the Soul of the World: Our Living Bond with Nature's Intelligence*, p. 102; Richard Tarnas, *The Passion of the Western Mind*, p. 213.
5. Giordano Bruno, *Cause, Principle, and Unity*, trans. Jack Lindsay, p. 81.
6. Alchemical text quoted by C. G. Jung, *Collected Works*, vol. 8, p. 388.
7. C. G. Jung, *Collected Works*, vol. 14, p. 372.
8. See John Eberly, *Al-Kimia: The Mystical Islamic Essence of the Sacred Art of Alchemy*.
9. *The Hermetic Museum*, 1:13, quoted by Edward Edinger in *The Anatomy of the Psyche*, p. 11. See also Vaughan-Lee, *Catching the Thread*, p. 66ff.
10. Quoted by Edinger, *Anatomy of the Psyche*, p. 231. Hermes Trismegistos is the "patron" of the alchemical art. According to legend, the original *Emerald Tablet* was found in the tomb of Hermes Trismegistos by Alexander the Great. "It is the cryptic epitome of the alchemical *opus*, a recipe for the second creation of the world, the *unus mundus*."
11. *Poems and Prose of Gerard Manley Hopkins*, "God's Grandeur."
12. Ghalib, trans. Jane Hirshfield, *The Enlightened Heart: An Anthology of Sacred Poetry*, ed. Stephen Mitchell, p. 105.
13. C. G. Jung, *Collected Works*, vol. 11, p. 759.
14. David Fideler, *Restoring the Soul of the World: Our Living Bond with Nature's Intelligence*, p. 78.
15. http://en.wikipedia.org/wiki/The_Garden_of_Cyrus.
16. Paul Oskar Kristeller, *The Philosophy of Marsilio Ficino*, p. 120.
17. Hermes Trismegistos, *The Emerald Tablet*, 4 & 5.
18. "Therefore you should carefully test and examine the life, character, and mental aptitude of any person who would be initiated in this Art." *The Hermetic Museum*, 2:12. Quoted by Edward Edinger, *Anatomy of the Psyche*, p. 7.
19. E. E. Cummings, "i thank You God for most this amazing," *Selected Poems 1923-1958*.

CH 6: THE LIGHT OF THE HEART

1. *Three Early Sufi Texts*, p. 52.
2. Some teachings say that the spiritual heart is in the center of the chest, while Sufis usually describe it as being on the left side, where the physical heart is. There is also a teaching that we have two hearts: the individual spiritual heart on the left side of the chest; while the cosmic, or *atmic* heart, is on the right side.
3. C. G. Jung, *Collected Works*, vol. 14, *Mysterium Coniunctionis*, ¶ 554.
4. William Chittick, *The Sufi Path of Knowledge*, p. 17.
5. *Katha Upanishad*, Book II, 1, *Ten Principle Upanishads*, trans. Shree Purohit Swami and W. B. Yeats, p. 34.
6. *Three Early Sufi Texts*, p. 35.
7. There are also five centers that belong to the physical world. Naqshbandis differentiated among five *latâ'if* belonging to the world of God's command (*'âlâm-e amr*)—heart (*qalb*), spirit (*rûh*), secret (*sirr*), hidden (*khafî*), and most hidden (*akhfâ*)—and five *latâ'if* belonging to the world of creation (*âlâm-e kalq*)—self (*nafs*), air (*hâd*), fire (*nâr*), water (*mâ*), and earth (*khâk*). Each *latîfah* is associated with a color and a specific location in the body.
8. Arthur F. Buehler, *Sufi Heirs of the Prophet*, p. 110.
9. Bhai Sahib, quoted in *Daughter of Fire: A Diary of a Spiritual Training With a Sufi Master*, by Irina Tweedie, p. 180.
10. The archetypal or symbolic world is traditionally seen as an intermediary plane between the physical world of the senses and the world of the soul, the plane of pure being. It is most easily accessed through the faculty of "active" or "creative" imagination. See Vaughan-Lee, *Working with Oneness*, ch. 8: "Imagination," pp. 111–124.

CH 7: THE AXIS OF LOVE

1. Quoted by Claude Addas, "The Experience and Doctrine of Love in Ibn 'Arabî," *Sufi*, Issue 63, Autumn 2004, p. 24.
2. This is similar to Brother Lawrence's "Practice of the Presence of God," except that it focuses on the awareness of the heart and the presence of divine love.
3. See Vaughan-Lee, *The Signs of God*, in particular the final chapter, "Recognizing the Signs of God."
4. See Vaughan-Lee, *In the Company of Friends*.
5. See Vaughan-Lee, *Spiritual Power*, ch. 7: "The Language of Love," pp. 120–141.

BIBLIOGRAPHY

Addas, Claude. "The Experience and Doctrine of Love in Ibn 'Arabî," *Sufi*, Issue 63, Autumn 2004.

Brother Lawrence. *The Practice of the Presence of God*. London: Samuel Badger and Sons.

Bruno, Giordano. *Cause, Principle, and Unity: Five Dialogues*. Trans. Jack Lindsay. New York: International Publishers, 1964.

Buehler, Arthur F. *Sufi Heirs of the Prophet*. Columbia, SC: University of South Carolina, 1998.

Chittick, William. *The Sufi Path of Knowledge*. Albany, NY: State University of New York Press, 1989.

Church, David, ed. *Healing the Heart of the World*. Santa Rosa, CA: Elite Books, 2010.

Corbin, Henry. *Creative Imagination in the Sufism of Ibn 'Arabi*. Princeton: Princeton University Press, 1969.

Cummings, E. E. *Selected Poems 1923–1958*. London: Faber and Faber, 1960.

Douglas-Klotz, Neil. *Desert Wisdom: A Nomad's Guide to Life's Big Questions from the Heart of the Native Middle East*. Worthington, OH: ARC Books and Abwoon Network, 2011.

Eberly, John. *Al-Kimia*. Hillsdale, NY: Sophia Perennis, 2004.

Edinger, Edward. *Anatomy of the Psyche*. La Salle, IL: Open Court Publishing, 1985.

Eisenstein, Charles. *Climate: A New Story*. Berkeley, CA: North Atlantic Books, 2018.

Fideler, David. *Restoring the Soul of the World: Our Living Bond with Nature's Intelligence*. Rochester, VT: Inner Traditions, 2014.

Harvey, Andrew. *Light Upon Light: Inspirations from Rumi*. Berkeley: North Atlantic Books, 1996.

Hoeller, Stephan. *Gnosis: A Journal of Western Inner Traditions*, vol. 8, Summer 1988.

Holy Bible, Authorized Version. London: 1611.

Hopkins, Gerard Manley. *The Poems and Prose of Gerard Manley Hopkins*. Harmondsworth: Penguin Books, 1953.

Jung, C. G. *Collected Works*. London: Routledge & Kegan Paul.

Kingsley, Peter. *Reality*. Inverness, CA: The Golden Sufi Center, 2004.

Kristeller, Paul Oskar. *Philosophy of Marsilio Ficino*. New York: Columbia University Press, 1984.

Mitchell, Stephen, ed. *The Enlightened Heart: An Anthology of Sacred Poetry*. New York: Harper & Row, 1989.

Plato. *Plato's Timaeus*. Trans. F. M. Cornford. Indianapolis, IN: Bobbs-Merrill, 1959.

Razî, Najm al-Dîn. *The Path of God's Bondsmen*. Trans. Hamid Algar. North Haledon, NJ: Islamic Publications International, 1980.

Tirmidhî, al-Hakîm al-. *Three Early Sufi Texts*. Trans. Nicholas Heer. Louisville, KY: Fons Vitae, 2003.

Tweedie, Irina. *Daughter of Fire: A Diary of a Spiritual Training with a Sufi Master*. Nevada City, CA: Blue Dolphin Publishing, 1986.

Vaughan-Lee, Llewellyn. *Darkening of the Light: Witnessing the End of an Era*. Point Reyes, CA: The Golden Sufi Center, 2013.

—. *For Love of the Real: A Story of Life's Mystical Secret*. Point Reyes, CA: The Golden Sufi Center, 2015.

—. *In the Company of Friends*. Point Reyes, CA: The Golden Sufi Center, 1994.

—. *Signs of God*. Point Reyes, CA: The Golden Sufi Center, 2001.

—. *Spiritual Power: How It Works*. Point Reyes, CA: The Golden Sufi Center, 2005; second edition, 2019.

—. *Working with Oneness*. Point Reyes, CA: The Golden Sufi Center, 2002.

Wohlleben, Peter. *The Hidden Life of Trees*. Trans. Jane Billinghurst. Vancouver, BC: Greystone Books, 2016.

Yeats, W. B. *Collected Poems of W. B. Yeats*. London: Macmillan, 1933.

—. *The Ten Principal Upanishads*. Trans. (with Shree Purohit Swami). London: Faber and Faber, 1937.

INDEX

ACKNOWLEDGMENTS

For permission to use copyrighted material, the author gratefully wishes to acknowledge: Liveright Publishing Corporation, for permission to quote lines from "i thank You God for most this amazing". Copyright 1950, © 1978, 1991 by the Trustees for the E. E. Cummings Trust. Copyright © 1979 by George James Firmage, from *Complete Poems: 1904–1962* by E. E. Cummings, edited by George J. Firmage; Islamic Publications International for excerpts from *The Path of God's Bondsmen* by Najm al-Dîn Razî, translated by Hamid Algar © 1980 Center for Iranian Studies, Columbia University; Dr. Neil Douglas-Klotz, for the selection from "The Mother Womb Creates the Human (Babylonian-Assyrian)" from *Desert Wisdom: A Nomad's Guide to Life's Big Questions from the Heart of the Native Middle East*, copyright © 2011 Neil Douglas-Klotz. Reprinted with permission. All rights reserved. Information: ARC Books and Abwoon Network: www.abwoon.org; Jane Hirshfield, for the lines from "Even at prayer, our eyes look inward," from *The Enlightened Heart: An Anthology of Sacred Poetry*, ed. Stephen Mitchell: Copyright © 1989 by Jane Hirshfield.

Interior image: Nine Choirs of Angels, from the *Liber Scivias (Know the Ways of the Lord)* by German mystic St. Hildegaard of Bingen (1098–1179).

Cover art: Original collage by Anat Vaughan-Lee, with images used under license from Shutterstock.com: *Planet earth with a spectacular sunset* by solar seven/shutterstock.com (photo ID: 70269238); and *Hands of a young woman in praying position over a dark background* by ptnphoto/shutterstock.com (photo ID: 172424882).

ABOUT *the* AUTHOR

LLEWELLYN VAUGHAN-LEE, Ph.D., is a Sufi teacher in the Naqshbandiyya-Mujaddidiyya Sufi Order. Born in London in 1953, he has followed the Naqshbandi Sufi path since he was nineteen. In 1991 he moved to Northern California and founded The Golden Sufi Center (www.goldensufi.org).

He has authored a series of books that give a detailed exploration of the stages of spiritual and psychological transformation experienced on the Sufi path, with a particular focus on the use of dreamwork as inner guidance on the journey. Since 2000 the focus of his writing and teaching has been on spiritual responsibility in our present time of transition, the awakening global consciousness of oneness, and spiritual ecology (www.workingwithoneness.org). He has also been featured in the TV series *Global Spirit* and was interviewed by Oprah Winfrey as a part of her *Super Soul Sunday* series.

ABOUT *the* PUBLISHER

THE GOLDEN SUFI CENTER is a California Religious Non-Profit Corporation dedicated to making the teachings of the Naqshbandi Sufi path available to all seekers. For further information about the activities and publications, please contact:

THE GOLDEN SUFI CENTER
P.O. Box 456
Point Reyes, CA 94956
tel: 415-663-0100 · *fax:* 415-663-0103
www.goldensufi.org